WHAT THE BIBLE INTENDS TO SAY

Goals and Guidelines for Proper Biblical Interpretation

BARRY L. CALLEN

ALDERSGATE PRESS

WHAT THE BIBLE INTENDS TO SAY

GOALS AND GUIDELINES FOR PROPER BIBLICAL INTERPRETATION

BY BARRY L. CALLEN

PUBLISHED BY:

ALDERSGATE **PRESS**

The publications arm of

WESLEYAN
HOLINESS
CONNECTION

HOLINESSANDUNITY.ORG

IN COLLABORATION WITH:

LAMP POST
publishers

lamppostpublishers.com

Printed in the United States of America

Soft Cover ISBN 13:   978-1-60039-318-1
ebook ISBN-13:   978-1-60039-990-9

WHAT THE BIBLE INTENDS TO SAY

"Barry Callen offers helpful guidance that focuses on readers becoming listeners to the Spirit's voice through Scripture. He provides useful correction to persons who cite the Bible to support beliefs and practices hurtful in church life. Here are approaches to Bible reading that yield intended wisdom for living in our contemporary world. This is a must read for church people!"

Dr. Richard P. Thompson, Director, Wesley Center Online,
Northwest Nazarene University

"The noise of modern life overshadows the wisdom of the ages. A return to Scripture was never more vital. Barry Callen's crucial invitation is to embrace the Bible as a living testimony meant to transform our hearts and minds. In an age of biblical illiteracy and only a superficial engagement with spiritual matters, Callen awakens a reverence for the intended purpose of Scripture."

Bishop John Mark Richardson, Executive Director, Wesleyan Holiness Connection,
Regional Bishop of the Church of God in Christ

"The Bible is the divinely inspired revelation of God, the core of Christian understanding. A strength of Wesleyan-Holiness theology is its recognition of the dynamic intersection of human life and the voice of the Holy Spirit. Jesus promised that the Spirit "would teach you all things" (Jn 14:26). The Spirit is the optometrist of choice for clarifying our vision of the meaning and mystery of Scripture. Callen properly reminds us that our sanctification by the Spirit is required for sound biblical reading and understanding."

Rev. Jim Lyon, pastor, author, teacher, former General Director of Church of God
Ministries and President of the Global Wesleyan Alliance

"Here is a clear treatment of proper ways to understand intended biblical teaching. Focusing on the central role of the Holy Spirit in biblical inspiration and interpretation, Callen emphasizes the particular wisdom of the Wesleyan Holiness traditions of the faith. This book is valuable in university and local church contexts because its format and language do not presume prior knowledge of numerous scholarly issues."

Dr. Nathan Willowby, Dean, College of Christian Ministry, Music, and Theatre, and
Associate Professor of Theology and Ethics, Anderson University

CONTENTS

FOREWORD

Dr. Cheryl Bridges Johns, Distinguished Visiting Professor & Director of Pentecostal House of Study, United Theological Seminary. A celebrated author, she serves as a member of the Executive Board of the Association of Theological Schools in the United States and Canada, a member of the Executive Committee of the Commission on Faith and Order of the National Council of Churches and of the Board of Directors of the Wesleyan Holiness Connection.

It's not an exaggeration to say that we are in a crisis of biblical illiteracy. People spend more time watching T.V. and scrolling through social media than reading or listening to Scripture. The Bible no longer haunts us with its vivid stories and deep truths. This lack of attention to the Bible says much about the state of discipleship in Christian churches. Modern Christians have reduced the Bible's lively oracles to a flat, two-dimensional document containing facts and principles easily distilled and managed.

Wesleyans, birthed as a Spirit-led renewal movement, have not been immune to this sterile vision of the Bible. Everything, including the Bible, tends to get reduced to an objective landscape. We view the Bible as a mere book of facts and principles. I firmly believe that Wesleyanism can be a catalyst for another Great Awakening. However, such a deep renewal will not happen until we find a much greater love for Scripture and embrace it as conveying the *real divine presence.*

In my 2023 *Re-enchanting the Text: Discovering the Bible as Sacred, Dangerous, and Mysterious,* I offer a way of viewing the biblical text as a holy space that radiates the real presence of God's triune life. Now comes this book in which Dr. Barry L. Callen effectively offers and develops well a similar vision of the Bible.

For him, the Bible should be read through the eyes of the Spirit. He contends that this is the way Jesus read Scripture. "It's the presence of the Spirit that turns mere reading of the biblical text into a potentially life-changing experience. The Spirit of God enables movement from textual scanning to Spirit living."

Callen encourages readers to embrace a biblical world "that is alive and reaching for the reader by the Spirit." The reader is invited to respond to this outreach, not by standing at an objective and safe distance, but by standing *within* and *under* the text. For Callen, reading is to be done in a "relational mode, prayerfully, obediently, in conversation with the church of yesterday, and considering all knowledge from any source."

Such a humble, relational reading posture does not negate careful study and investigation of the original intent of the biblical passages. What it does offer is much more, a "surplus of meaning." Callen presents clear and thoughtful guidelines for biblical interpretation that honor four critical assumptions.

The reading focus is to be: (1) on the Bible we *now possess,* not on a theorized "autograph" we don't have; (2) on *what the Bible intends to say,* not what we want it to say; (3) on *the whole* of the inspired biblical text, not verses that yield false messages when forced to stand alone; and (4) on awareness that *knowing and practicing* the faith are closely related.

I believe you will find this book life-changing. It's written clearly and sensitively. It creates a powerful hunger for the life-giving Word of God and charts the proper path for entering the sacred biblical world as God surely intends.

FOREWORD

Dr. Ryan Danker, Director of the John Wesley Institute. He formerly taught on the faculties of Wesley Theological Seminary and Greensboro College. His ecumenical efforts have included serving on the United Methodist-Roman Catholic Dialogue. He now is a member of the Board of Directors of the Wesleyan Holiness Connection and of the Board of Advisors of the WHC's Aldersgate Press.

One of the many gifts of the Wesleyan renewal in eighteenth-century England was a clear love for the Scripture as a "means of grace," a channel of God's very presence and power. John Wesley was formed in the tradition of the Church of England where a critical prayer was appointed for the second Sunday in Advent.

This Advent prayer asks that God enable the faithful to truly encounter Scripture, to "hear, read, mark, learn, and inwardly digest" so that "by patience and comfort of Thy holy Word we may embrace the blessed hope of everlasting life given in Christ."

John Wesley wrote eloquently about the beauty of Scripture in the preface to his *Notes Upon the New Testament*:

In the language of the sacred writings, all the elegancies of human composures sink into nothing before it: God speaks, not as man, but as God. His thoughts are very deep, and thus His words are of inexhaustible virtue.

God's Word written provides a personal encounter with Christ. Recapturing the beauty of Scripture means recapturing the power of encounter, Christ's life in us. The early Methodists led by the Wesley brothers had a clear mission, "to reform the nation, particularly the church, and the spread scriptural holiness over the land." This was a scriptural renewal movement centered in spiritual encounter that was biblically inspired.

Among the means of grace is what John Wesley called "meditating on Scripture." This is more than a cursory reading but an engagement with the Bible that opens the believer to the very work of God described in its pages. Such reading necessarily involves meeting Christ and receiving his very life.

In *What the Bible Means to Say,* Dr. Barry Callen reminds us of what the Bible is truly intended to say and do. It's to enable an actual encounter with the living God. The Bible is no dead book, even though written and compiled so long ago. It speaks to us every time we open it if we are truly seeking the One who inspired its original writing and now inspires its contemporary reading.

Unlike most authors, Callen has intentionally written a book that will lead the reader to another one, the Bible itself. When a reader follows Callen's lead, that reader will be armed with the interpretation insights of a faithful scholar who speaks for Jesus. The point of this book and of the Bible itself is new life *in Christ.* That's what the Bible is intending to say!

Says Callen, "The divine dynamics of Pentecost fuse the past dealings of God with humanity and the present possibilities of dramatic new life and mission. Sharing in these dynamics is how to read the Bible in depth. On that first Pentecost, the disciples of Jesus had their tongues loosed and found flames dancing on their heads (Acts 2). Real reading of God's written Word allows it to come alive and begin to read and alter the reader!"

For such critical wisdom so needed by the church today, this book is to be commended indeed.

PREFACE

We dare not confuse becoming an expert in biblical trivia with a faithful reading of what the Bible intends to teach. The Bible isn't merely a book full of bits of incidental information of eternal wisdom on countless subjects about which we might be curious. Instead, it's *Scripture*, that is, it conveys a divine message that intends to transform life itself. More than a human production, the Bible is the book of the Spirit of God.

To read the Bible as Scripture is more complex than casually roaming through a supposed religious encyclopedia for something of current interest. Being able to list the twelve most prominent biblical mountains and the names and spellings of the Jewish kings and minor prophets is far less important than engaging in the Bible's real goal. We are to read in order to hear the voice of God's Spirit through the Bible's text and thereby be changed into the image of Jesus Christ!

Reading the Bible properly necessarily involves allowing it *to read us.* The Bible is primarily about Jesus coming, teaching dying, and rising on our behalf. The intention of reading it is to change anyone who comes to understand who Jesus is and who then we can become. This intended change is a spiritual transformation by the power of the Spirit of Jesus. Quality Bible reading leads to being increasingly re-formed by the Father, through the Son, according to the work of the Spirit. The recorded story of God *with* us is intended to enable a new reality of God *in* us and then *through* us.

Reading and interpreting the Bible properly necessarily will be oriented around the past and present ministry of the Spirit of God. The divine revelation comes through more than reading the words of the biblical pages, as though they themselves are the inerrant records direct from the mouth of God. Should such literary perfection have been intended by God, Jesus would have come in the age of audio and video recording when nothing of his would have been lost, mistaken, or taken out of context.

In fact, Jesus came far sooner than our digital days. To our knowledge, he never spoke the language in which his life and teachings were recorded. The recording of them that we have was done with four Gospels that are hardly mirror images of each other. Nonetheless, believers are instructed to accept by faith that God's Spirit was at work "inspiring" the biblical writers, editors, and compilers, and now works to unfold the truth for us, the modern readers.

God has chosen to breathe into these biblical documents. This breathing transforms them into dependable carriers of the wisdom of God. They rise above being merely products of human composers to also being *sufficient* for our saving knowledge of Jesus.

Paul declared in 2 Timothy 3:16 that "all Scripture" is inbreathed with the life of the Spirit. Therefore, all of it is adequate and useful for our instruction in spiritual living. Of course, Paul was referring only to the Old Testament materials he knew as a trained Jew. A few generations after Paul, the Christian community came to consensus about an additional group of documents judged equally inbreathed, worthy, and useful. They now are known as the New Testament.

Here we will refer to these Testaments as *Foundational* and *Final*. This is because "Old" unfairly suggests outdated and no longer useful and "New" has deep roots in the "Old" often unrecognized. The second is difficult to understand without the first and the first is incomplete without the second.

The Bible as we now have it should be received as the primary source of divinely inspired instruction for Christians. Even so, we are faced with the many challenges of interpretation that require thoughtful understandings of the Bible's goals and the reader's adherence to needed guidelines that steer away from serious misunderstandings.

Abraham Lincoln observed a great irony in his second inaugural address as president. The terrible Civil War had been fueled in part by both sides reading the same Bible and getting from it very different messages. How could that be? Disaster often follows when the goals and guidelines of biblical interpretation are twisted or ignored.

Church history is littered with Christians burning heretics, launching crusades seeking to regain holy sites by force, supporting human slavery, suppressing women, displacing native peoples in the name of cultural progress, and more. All this was justified by use of misread verses or passages of the Bible. We need the Bible and help in reading it correctly.

The conclusion? "Only converted people can be entrusted with inspired writings. They alone are less likely to use the Bible as a rationale for their bad behavior."[1] "Converted" here means more than being a church member who repeats an "orthodox" creed and seeks to follow the rules of the church attended. It means a believer who is being obedient to the Spirit of God as the Spirit actively ministers divine truth through the biblical text into contemporary applications.

To what end does the Spirit of God work? The Spirit seeks to continue the teaching of Jesus and reform every believer into a

Bible reader who increasingly reflects the image of Jesus Christ to the world. The wise Christian must learn how to read the Bible with the Spirit. If the ministry of the Spirit is not honored in the reading and interpreting of the biblical text, the result likely will be toxic. That's the last thing God wants or this troubled world needs.

Let's learn to read the Bible through the eyes and for the purposes of the Spirit. This follows the pattern of Jesus himself. He was anything but a literalist, legalist, or slave to mere words of the Scripture he knew or to the traditional teachings by the elders that he often contested. Rather, he taught as he understood his Father to be directing. A good first interpretive principle is to follow how Jesus handled Scripture.

The Bible reports many historical events. Our task is to discover the ongoing message of that reporting for our time. Jesus shows us what to see in the reporting, what to emphasize and deemphasize or even ignore. A key skill is learning to distinguish between what the Bible may only *report* and what it intentionally *teaches*.

Our Lord "read the inspired text in an inspired way. He had an eye for identifying which passages were creating a highway for God and which were merely cultural, self-serving, and legalistic additions."[2] Our learning to read the Bible must involve proceeding in the manner of our Lord. It's his written Word and his Spirit will be our guide.

Prior to his bodily departure after the resurrection, Jesus promised his disciples, now us, that all his teachings and their fuller meanings and applications would be provided in the future *by his Spirit* (Jn 14:26). To that Spirit we now seek to listen with care as we learn how to read the inspired book of God.

Barry L. Callen

Fall, 2025

WHAT THE BIBLE INTENDS TO SAY

Goals and Guidelines for Proper Biblical Interpretation

1

READING MOTIVES AND CHALLENGES

Why read the Bible? We fallen humans need dependable wisdom from God. God makes it uniquely available in one collection of written materials as in no other. Even so, the nature, age, length, languages, and organization of the Bible combine to make its contemporary interpretation a difficult challenge. What the Bible is understood to be saying depends in part on what knowledge and motives the reader brings to the reading.

The Bible is a complex, long, and ancient piece of literature. It was written by numerous authors and then arranged later by editors. Its several original languages are not known by the typical modern reader. Accurate current understanding of its central themes and overall goals requires careful attention to a series of rules of interpretation.[3]

Giving attention to these rules is very important, and yet this is not the main burden of this book. What often is overlooked is the ministry of the Spirit of God that is critical to the intended impact of the written Word on the understanding and life of today's reader.

Ancient inspiration of the biblical text by the Spirit of God is to be affirmed and then matched by awareness of the contemporary illumination by the same Spirit for the reader. The ancient writer was in need of the Spirit's assistance, and so is the modern reader.

Maybe only the "converted" can be trusted with biblical interpretation. The Spirit-lacking person can read with the best of literary tools of evaluation and still miss the deepest points being made. A doctorate in theology or the holding of some high position in a church establishment is no guarantee that an "official" interpretation is the final word on "what the Bible says."

Focus on God's Intention

Today's followers of Jesus need a deep immersion into God's Word as written. Their reading must be infused with the interpretive presence of the Spirit of Jesus. It's the presence of this Spirit that turns mere reading of the biblical text into a potentially life-changing experience. The Spirit of God enables movement from textual scanning to Spirit living.

The Spirit seeks to enable a transformative encounter and ongoing relational intimacy between God and reader. Spiritual *being* is required for insightful Bible reading. Both must come before "religious" *doing* is possible for a true Christian.

The goal of Bible reading isn't speed or volume of pages covered so much as depth of Spirit hearing that leads to obeying the voice of God coming through the written Word. Instructs Paul, "Finally, brothers and sisters, whatever is true, whatever is noble, whatever is right, whatever is pure, whatever is lovely, whatever is admirable— if anything is excellent or praiseworthy—*think about such things*"

(Phil. 4:8). Read and think with mind and heart open to the voice of the Spirit and the potential reality of new life in the Spirit arising from inspired biblical understandings.

Two motives for Bible reading are common, with one clearly best. There is the surface reading motive that's primarily "informational." The reader is looking for choice religious quotes or concepts that satisfy curiosity and fill out teaching outlines or sermon manuscripts or seems to answer someone's pressing question.

The second approach, the one urged here, assumes that God is seeking to *read the reader,* change a person in the reading encounter. The Bible is the medium that carries God's presence and message of spiritual change. It's the arena of Divine-human encounter where the Spirit engages the reader and activates change that then motivates mission.

There are clear challenges to the success of such Bible reading. The Bible is comprised of sixty-six separate "books." This mass of material isn't always arranged chronologically or often even by themes. Some of it goes into detail about matters that now appear outdated. Historical reports get repeated by different writers with slightly different slants and even contrasting information on the same thing.

If God were to have written this book apart from human authors and editors, surely it would have a more consistent style, no contrasts of viewpoint, no long sections of ancient history that modern readers won't understand, and numerous footnotes needed to explain the most obscure things included for unknown reasons. If God submitted the present biblical writing as a proposed Ph.D. dissertation, it surely would fail the test.

Fortunately, God is in no need of a doctorate and many human authors and editors clearly were involved. Let's open this book believing that God waits in it for our arrival. Let's read, determined to be open to the voice of the Spirit and willing to be made new in the image of Jesus Christ.

You are invited to enroll in the best of spiritual schools and seek the highest of its degrees. Your tuition, costly indeed, already has been paid. The school is the Bible, the lead teacher the Spirit of God, and the curriculum built around acceptance of the "Scripture Principle." It's this.

> The "Scripture Principle" is the assertion that the Bible is the primary and fully trustworthy canon of Christian revelation, the reliable medium for encountering and understanding the God who seeks to transform all persons who read the sacred text into the image of Jesus Christ. It's the belief that Scripture never leads one astray in regard to what it intentionally teaches.[4]

This belief separates from any Christian "conservatism" that claims more for the Bible than the Bible claims for itself. It also is a caution about any Christian "liberalism" that tends to undercut biblical authority in favor of contemporary thinking based on non-biblical assumptions. The result we seek is solid ground that retains strong biblical authority in relation to that which the Bible *intends to teach*.

Amazing World of the Bible

The Bible is lengthy, old, and originally written in at least three non-English languages. It comes to a contemporary reader through a parade of authors, editors, editions, and translations, with many variations of textual layout and claimed interpretations. Even so, reading it with care is more than worth the time. Necessary assistance is needed and available.

Why read despite the challenges? The Bible is the primary medium for the revelation of God to us today. It's difficulties pale in comparison to the great benefits to be gained. The Bible is nothing less than "the autobiography of the pioneer people of God in their pilgrimage of faith. It is the standard for establishing norms of faith and the foundational material for treatises of faith" (theological belief statements).[5]

While sometimes tedious, the Bible is hardly dull. There's a talking donkey, a sperm-free pregnancy, God telling his prophet to marry a practicing prostitute, a little diarrhea shown to be associated with bringing on romance, and an apparent flying saucer that may have been God once visiting Earth.

We meet a queen parading nude in public, except for her crown, and a peg driven through a sleeping guy's head by the very hostess who had just served him the best of dinners. The Bible begins with everything coming from nothing and ends with beasts and dragons setting the stage for the skies to open wide at the end of time.

A baby is born in a barn. Between diaper changes, he frightens a king so badly that the powerful man orders all babies in town killed to be sure he gets this one who is so dangerous![6] Baby Jesus was missed in this horrible chaos. He grew up thrilling crowds and angering established religion leaders. Then he was murdered on false charges. Jesus had turned out to be all that had been so feared, head of a new "kingdom" not of this world, one that most people couldn't understand and none could control.

After his murder, Jesus forgot to stay in his tomb. This so inspired a few unlettered friends of his that they proceeded to turn the world on its head! Jesus published nothing, led no army in revolution, and founded no new religion. And yet, somehow, it's widely assumed that he is the most important man to have ever lived.

Is this the stuff of human imagination out of control or the most amazing and wonderful story ever told? Was Jesus more than just another man? Dare to read the Bible with care, listen to the Spirit, and risk being changed and inflamed yourself.

As the amazing biblical story goes, Jesus was in existence before the original creation and now has ascended to heaven and promises to be with believers until the end of time and beyond. He claimed to be God actually with us fallen humans. Should this be true, he is the only real hope for humanity. All dimensions of his story should demand our utmost attention. This calls for Bible reading necessarily assisted by the Spirit of Jesus.

We humans can't settle for some people thinking of Jesus as only the greatest teacher who ever was. After all, he claimed to be the center of his own teaching and the pinnacle of all human history. Either Jesus was indeed *God with us* or he was a lunatic who deserved to be put away. These are the only logical options. Read the Bible that tells it all. Judge for yourself. Read with an open heart listening for the voice of the Spirit of God. Risk finding yourself being read by the Spirit and changed!

Good Bible reading should reflect the experience of those early Christian disciples at Pentecost. Their perspectives changed rapidly because, to use Final Testament adjectives, they were "bewildered," "puzzled," and "astonished" (Acts 2:12). They found themselves thinking and acting differently, reading all reality in fresh ways. They had been read themselves and had become different people. God was present, speaking, acting, changing things.

Analyzing the biblical text in "literary-critical" ways can help reveal the Spirit's working. However, doing this in the sterile environment of mere literary probing can be counter-productive. It's then only an academic exercise of technical research carried on at a safe distance. Such is done in some schools today as "The Bible as Literature." Entering the biblical world that is alive and reaching for the reader by the Spirit is quite another thing.

The divine dynamics of Pentecost tend to fuse the whole of the past dealings of God with humanity and the present possibilities of dramatic new life and mission. Sharing in these divine dynamics is how to read the Bible in depth. According to the Book of Acts, on that first Pentecost the disciples of Jesus suddenly realized that their tongues were loosed and divine flames were dancing on their heads (Acts 2). That's real reading of God's Word as it becomes alive and begins to read and alter the reader! Are you willing to take such a risk?

God's Word Written

The Bible is not the "Word of God" in the same way as is Jesus Christ. It's not a book of magic, divine literature that itself is to be worshiped. Humans wrote it and it reflects their cultures and personalities and sometimes literary frailties. This human dimension of the Bible, however, does *not* require throwing the "baby out with the bathwater." It requires only that we take the Bible for what it claims to be, not what we insist it must be or we can't believe anything it says.

As a book of Divine-human partnership, the Bible is our primary witness to Jesus Christ. When interpreted correctly, it's our primary authority for Christian faith and practice. It's "the cradle that holds the Christ child" (Martin Luther) even though it does not answer every question life brings.

Faith in Jesus Christ will come through a combination of our reading the Bible and the current ministry of the Spirit of Jesus who is anxious to communicate Jesus to us through the words of the Bible. Our eyes will need special vision provided only through the eyes of the Spirit. True understanding of biblical writings depends finally on our encounter with Jesus Christ and the inner testimony of the Spirit of God in connection with the Bible's many and quite diverse materials.

There is no need for an awkward choice between theological "fundamentalism" and "liberalism."[7] They are opposite extremes of contemporary reaction to the truth perversions of modern times. Instead of these extremes, we return to the Hebrew roots of Christian faith that yield a more balanced and fruitful understanding of the Word of God written. The Bible's ongoing meaning is provided by God most fully to those restored in the image of the Son by the power of the Spirit.

2

BECOMING CAPTIVE TO THE WORD

"All scripture is inspired by God and is useful for teaching" (2 Tim 3:16).

"The Word of God is living and active, sharper than any two-edged sword" (Matt 5:17; Heb 4:12).

"We tear down arguments and every presumption set up against the knowledge of God and take captive every thought to make it obedient to Christ" (2 Cor 10:5).

A new era of Christianity began with an obscure Roman Catholic priest in Germany. Martin Luther was refusing to recant his new and beliefs about the Christian faith. They were highly unacceptable to the church of the time. Born a peasant in 1483, by the year 2000 Luther carried the title "Man of the Millennium." This Christian theologian and reformer had been judged by a modern secular magazine the most influential human of the last 1,000 years!

What did Luther do that was so important? He nailed to his church door in Germany a protest of "95 Theses." They dared announce things so threatening to his church inquisitors that his very life was brought into question. Regardless, he announced, "My conscience is *captive to the Word of God*, bound by the Scriptures."

Young Luther had been freed by a grand amazement. He had discovered that there is a path to human salvation beyond human obedience to church dictates. It's the biblical path. Salvation is *by faith alone*. We humans don't work to earn our way to heaven. Christ already has paved the way.

Luther was breaking from the authority of the Pope of Rome and the church Councils that were in full control of official Christian thinking at the time. His new loyalty was to the revealed Word of God as written and ministered by the Spirit. This daringly independent stance ignited a revolution in the Western world, upsetting the church and the related religious and political commitments of many nations.

There even was his translation of the Bible into a language common people could read. Direct access to the biblical text further tended to undermine church control of religious and public affairs. This priest was helping the average believer to read and interpret for themselves and be captive only to what they understood the Bible to say.

Two Critical Assumptions

#1 The Bible We Have. Two critical assumptions need immediate clarity for Bible reading today. Focus should be on the Bible *we now possess* and on that Bible being understood as *the transforming medium of the saving message of God*. This first assumption recognizes that God has not provided the church with a Bible that is a perfect literary document in the sense that we now might define "perfect." Instead, the church has been blessed with a Bible believed to be fully authoritative and quite sufficient as it is when received and interpreted properly in relation to its intended purpose.

Not helpful is the recent assumption of some that biblical authority will emerge only from an "inerrant autograph," a supposed perfect biblical text originally existing but unseen by any of us. Ancient Bible-related documents now have been discovered that have brought new light to old Bible-related texts and issues, light not available to translators, editors, and readers of earlier generations. Even so, while still lacking literary perfection, we may proceed in confidence with what we have.

Numerous translations of the Bible's text have been produced to better clarify what likely were the ancient meanings of languages now known only by linguistic specialists. Archaeological discoveries have enabled fresh understandings of how the Bible came about and precisely what it apparently means at various points. The few remaining literary imperfections are incidental and insignificant. The Bible in our hands is fully sufficient for its God-given purpose. It's read best by the present guidance of the originating Spirit of God.

God's Spirit ministers biblical truth within the church and is the intended conversation partner of every Bible reader. In addition, "the church historic and global provides conversation partners 'not like us' who can assist in hearing those melodies in Scripture for which we would otherwise have no ear."[8] Rather than diversity in the church being a danger, it's a valuable resource for biblical interpretation.

The Bible never leads one astray in regard to what it intentionally teaches. Our believing captivity as Christians is not to things incidental within its text. Staying focused keeps one from getting lost. Below will be detailed those matters that should be the reader's focus of attention.

The Bible is not a comprehensive encyclopedia of all religious and secular knowledge, including wisdom on many modern issues of astronomy, geology, psychology, genetics, evolution, sociology, etc. Instead, the Bible is all that it claims to be and not the more that some modern humans wish it were and sometimes wrongly believe it is.

We contemporary Bible readers are to become captive to the Spirit of God who once inspired the biblical text and now intends to illumine its current meanings and applications. Such captivity is the path to the real spiritual freedom, faith relevance, and joy in Christian believing and living.

#2 Christ-like Persons We Are To Be. The first assumption was about the nature of the Bible we now possess. Now for the second assumption needing clarity, the prime purpose of the Bible we now possess. The many biblical words and editions and translations are means and not the goal. God's inspiring intent is not that we all become textual technicians and doctrinal experts but *Christ-like persons*.

Reading the Bible properly is not merely analyzing the text and looking for assured information about God. It isn't simply locating a set of statements about God and rules for life. "It's a pathway into God's very life."[9] We read the Bible to be impacted by Christ's Spirit through the living *dynamic* of the biblical text, not through the fixedness of its every word.

The Bible is the transforming message of God. Words are fragile tools, human means to capture and convey reality that can't be contained fully in mere words. The Bible is the assured guide to understanding the *source* and *means* and *destiny* of human salvation. For this purpose it proves wholly sufficient.

The source of the Bible's best understanding is the present ministry of the revealing Spirit of God who carefully unfolds the biblical text within the remembering and reading church. The Spirit who once "inspired" the original composition of the biblical text (breathed life into it) now works to "illuminate" its meaning, breathing into us fresh understanding and relevant applications. The Bible's interpretive process is a delicate one and yet always capable of sharing of the very wisdom and life of God.

One grand truth always must be central. Jesus, *the* Word of God, was with God before creation's beginning and *was* God. And the Word became flesh and lived among us, and we have seen his glory, the glory of the Father's only Son, full of grace and truth (Jn 1:1, 14). Praise be to God who is the Word and comes to us through the medium of the written Word by the ministry of the Spirit. To that coming we would be captive!

Adding the Proper Adjective

I have sought for many years to approach the biblical material in fresh ways that open its message for today's readers and reestablish its continuing authority when the Bible is read carefully and interpreted properly. I began in the context of my own Christian tradition, joining Richard Thompson in editing *Bible Reading in Wesleyan Ways* (2004).

The scope broadened when I and my friend Clark Pinnock produced *The Scripture Principle* (2009). My *Beneath the Surface* (2012) seeks to recover the relevance of the Foundational (Old) Testament for Final (New) Testament believers, while *Bible Stories for Strong Stomachs* (2017) takes many of the most difficult Bible stories and shows how they can still speak with significance.

The two volumes of *A Year with Rabbi Jesus* (2021, 2022) feature Jesus speaking again, guiding readers through the whole of the Bible with himself the key to its best understanding.[10] Then *All of God's Word for All of My Needs* (2023) followed to open the whole Bible for readers across one Christian Year of guided reading. This comprehensive reading plan better enables a believer to mature into the full image of Jesus Christ. Now we address here the very nature of the Bible and the critical role of the Spirit of God in its proper interpretation.

A worthy adjective is to be kept in front of the word "orthodoxy," the correct thinking we assume to get from our Bible reading. Common ones unfortunately have been "dead," "inflexible," "narrow," even "uncharitable" to all believers who differ. An alternative suggestion is "generous." There is "a crucial difference between the truths of the Christian faith and their doctrinal formulations at any particular point in church history."[11] One must be careful to what one becomes captive.

My first professor of Bible at the graduate level impressed on me that "prophetic" Bible preaching today by popular personalities usually commits three errors of Bible interpretation. They ignore the bulk of the prophetic material, misjudge the primary mission of the biblical prophet, and confuse or ignore the key distinction between prophetism and apocalypticism.

He concluded with this. "The declaration of the divine Word of God is a terrible, awesome responsibility. Failing to use legitimate methods of interpretation easily leads to proclaiming merely a human word."[12] Some proclamation, captivating as it may be to enthralled crowds, is outright abuse of the Word of God. We must read, teach, and preach the Bible with thoughtful care!

Humility within ourselves and graciousness toward others are most proper attitudes.

Captured by What?

The Apostle Paul pointed the Corinthian believers to the critical task of biblical interpretation. They were to be "smashing warped philosophies, tearing down barriers erected against the truth of God, fitting every loose thought and emotion and impulse into the structure of life shaped by Christ" (2 Cor 10:5, *The Message*). What a task for them and us!

The attempt at proper biblical interpretation faces the large obstacle of getting beyond alien cultural values embedded in all readers by life settings and educations. These values often are a problem because they are not necessarily Christian and quietly control our reading, thinking, and acting. They lead down blind alleys without our even being aware.

There is no purely "objective" biblical interpretation. We subjects engage objects and tend to see them through our pre-trained personal eyes. The Bible, however, is not to be viewed as only an object available for our human mastery. Our cultural and historical contexts supply habits of mind that lead to particular ways of reading. We must seek freedom from this captivity and find our way into the *context of Christ* for the habits of mind that enable true biblical understanding.

Take a simple example. "Don't smoke, drink, cuss, or chew and don't run around with girls who do." This proverb helped define necessary moral conduct for many Christians in America for generations. After all, Paul did say that "bad company corrupts good character" (1 Cor 15:33). The particulars of acceptable entertainment and male-female relations, however, tend to change depending on the place and time of one's life.

Especially in the Southern portion United States a generation or two ago, playing "cards" was considered activity of the devil by many Christian believers. However, "as you moved north, playing cards became more and more acceptable. When you reached Minnesota, you might find bridge tournaments in church. Christians are tempted to believe *our* mores originate from the Bible, leading to misreading the text."[13]

Today's Bible readers probably haven't had occasion to consider the possible immorality of an act deeply troubling to some of the earliest Christians. Would your stomach churn with evil and be filled with guilt if you had swallowed well-cooked meat known to have been offered previously by someone to an idol? Christian stomachs did once churn and sharp disputes followed (1 Cor 8-10).

More recently and in a very different cultural context, what about owning stock in a large and very diversified company known to expend invested money in ways we would find intolerable personally? What of paying taxes used largely to stockpile lethal weapons? While seeking to be not of the world, we do live in it and must decide how to adjust to it. Today's is a very complex and interconnected world.

What assumptions and attitudes should now control Christian definitions of acceptable eating and playing and investing as believers? Where did they come from? Are they formed by Christ or the current culture? Have we found in the Bible what's not there? We are to be careful of who or what has captured our thinking, maybe causing us to claim that what you think is the only Christian way--and we have Bible verses to prove it!

The goal of Christian Bible reading is accepting and employing the proper captivity. Put most simply, it's Paul's personal testimony. "It is no longer I who live, but it is *Christ who lives in me*" (Gal 2:20).

3

ONE RARE ISLAND

We humans reach for what may be impossible to attain. Can the Mystery behind all mysteries be found? Where is the place where we can absorb freely the wonder of the revealed Mystery, not for mere analysis but for our own humble transformation? Is there such a Mystery and place of revelation?

Humans dream for what may be the impossible. It's that place of awe that goes beyond description and analysis to pure joy. "And when he heard the sailors' tales, he was seized with a marvelous desire to dwell in that Isle of the Blessed, to live quietly on a perfect island, freed from kings and ceaseless wars." The reference is to Sentinel Island in the Bay of Bengal. While appearing idyllic, it's anything but safe and outsiders rarely are seen and never welcomed.[14]

In every troubled time, we beleaguered humans long for some idyllic place of isolated retreat safe from it all. The Bible claims to be that place but doesn't function quite that way. It acknowledges all the trouble but doesn't seek to remove its arrivers from it. It sends readers into the world as loving change agents. We tend to prefer that Bible reading offer sudden exits to heaven or, like Jews in the time of Jesus, provide a messiah who will quickly eliminate all hated occupiers.

The Bible leads toward believers being triumphant while still in trouble. Here's the goal of this retreat. "If it is true that there is Someone in charge of the whole mystery of life and death, we can hardly expect to escape a sense of futility until we begin to see what He is like and what His purposes are."[15] That's what Bible reading is all about, knowing God who faces and resolves trouble.

There is one rare and wonderful place that's real, full of unclaimed treasurers, and very inviting indeed. Instead of an isolated island, it's a book, the book of God that contains all we could ever need or wish. There is one problem. Its valuable contents are available only if the book is received properly and lived faithfully. Let's find our way to that place.

"Back to the Blessed Old Bible!"

A call often heard today is "Back to the Blessed Old Bible." This is thought the sure way to recover the pure truths of God. This is the right goal, although achieving it requires more than merely "reading" the book and finding the truths prepackaged in our terms. One must read in a way that enables encountering and being re-formed by God's Spirit into the very image of Jesus. That changes everything.

Let's explore this strange land of the Bible. I recommend making it your primary itinerary. It's the place that can elevate life to what it should and can be. It's an allusive and yet very real place that exists almost anywhere when permitted. It's hard to describe and not known by many these days. The welcome sign is always out.

Even with its many difficulties, journeying into the Bible is well worth the effort. Be assured that God is waiting with arms open. If you don't want to be changed by your reading and aren't prepared for risks and challenges, don't bother landing on the enchanting biblical shores.

The Bible is not like any other place. We won't find its treasurers if we come as colonialists hoping to take over and claim territory for personal, national, or denominational purposes. We must come to these ancient pages as humble visitors anxious to learn and be changed by our arrival. Jesus stands on the rocky textual shoreline and wants each reader to become like him. His Spirit will be the sure guide and make it all possible.

God is waiting in the surf to hand arrivers the key to the book that can convey life's needed wisdom and change. The key is the interpreting Spirit of God. God never separates himself from the book of God's revelation. We cannot successfully read it "objectively." It's not an object we can control. If looking for bits of religious information for our personal use apart from a personal relationship with God, the Bible will be read falsely. It will never yield its treasures.

The Bible has no independent existence. We must not try managing it as a stand-alone artifact of ancient times waiting for our reading and rational analysis. If we see it as a detailed self-help guide for life in modern times, one we can sample and apply as most convenient, it will be an immediate dead letter in our hands. To read this sacred book as God wishes requires coming to know God humbly and listening to the divine voice that always seeks to emerge from within the written text.

To know God is the path to becoming more like God. Reading the Bible with the intention of coming to know and be changed by God is to have really arrived on the blessed island of hope. Being there brings the possibility of becoming a new participant in the divine life, a citizen of a kingdom not of this world. Reading rightly the book of God means allowing God to read and transform you, the reader.

The story of Christianity "moves from a focus on mystery in the classical period, to institution in the medieval era, to individualism in the Reformation era, to reason in the modern era, and now in the postmodern era trying to reach back to mystery."[16] Don't be distracted by this generalization. It does have meaning. Christians often filter their faith understandings through the culture and philosophy of their times. They then freeze-frame this supposed wisdom, making it the standard for how Christianity is to be judged in all times. The freeze-frame is even weaponized for use against others.

Most Protestants today root their faith understanding in some post-sixteenth century movement like the great reformers, pietism, revivalism, fundamentalism, pentecostalism, deism, etc. Each fits its time of origin, but none is the whole of Christian reality, none alone the shore on which we need to land and the image we are being called to become.

Now comes the call for a re-emphasis on the mystery behind Christian faith that transcends all epochs and fixations. This mystery involves a "re-enchanting" of the biblical text. What lies beyond the words on the biblical pages are actual encounters with the divine presence who is the foundation and final interpreter of all biblical words.[17] Going back to the Bible requires going back to the God behind the Bible.

What Is "Truth"?

Truth is more than words and concepts, ideas and theories, slogans and creeds. It's personal relationship, transformation, incarnation.

It's "Christ in you—the hope of glory" (Col 1:27). The Word and Spirit of God are inseparable. The Bible is not merely a mass of words and religious ideas from the long history of the Jewish-Christian faith tradition. It's rather that one place where we learn of God coming to us *in person*. Only in receiving this coming of Jesus that now remains by his Spirit is there discovery of the proper way to read the Bible, the way that leads to the wellspring of life.

The great mystery is Christ himself (Col 2:2) who came to earth to reveal the Father by his love and sacrifice (Phil 2:1-11). The hope is having intimate personal relationship with Christ through his Spirit. The proper way to read the Bible is to come to know Jesus through the reading. He is yet alive in the ministry of the Spirit. Proper reading is hearing God's voice speaking through the medium of the biblical text for the purpose of present transformation into the image of Christ.

We contemporary Bible readers must let go of our fixations on previous ideas, doctrines, and religious institutions. We must free ourselves for the fresh and dynamic understandings provided by relationship with the Spirit. The Spirit is the one rare island where the blessedness we seek is to be found. Typical assumptions are abandoned there. Special reading skills must be practiced to first arrive and safely remain.

Humans are more than bodies attached to brains. Theology is more than carefully crafted creeds for use by the brain. Peace and justice will not emerge from any amount of mere knowledge. The more we know the more we humans seem inclined to misuse knowledge in service of our greed. The spirit of the human must be nurtured, honored, and somehow re-formed. True wisdom lies somewhere beyond our computer files, professional titles, and statistical analyses. All of that is burdened with "fallen" dimensions.

Needed is actual residence on the rare island of the Spirit. Required there are humility, sensitive ears, patience, faith, and openness to new life in Jesus Christ. We must approach the biblical text with all these. The purpose of our arrival must go beyond fascination and curiosity and the tendency to manipulation. It's to be made new in Jesus Christ.[18]

God's truth transcends our rational categories and academic tools, valuable as often they are. The truth from above is fundamentally reasonable and yet thoroughly personal, moving beyond mere reason. To be understood, Bible reading must include voices past and present, local and global, East and West, as the Bible engages today's contextual challenges. God is still up to something important through Jesus Christ by the Spirit in the revealing written Word.

We often quote the Bible while knowing only what we think we know about its teaching. The Bible is a strange land where simple reading and quick believing and thoughtless applying require careful examination. To read God's Word properly, we need the help of the church of the ages, the best of present thinking, and the immediate voice of the Spirit.

With such combined assistance, the Bible can become an essential and reliable guide to the Christian life. When properly read, it's the record of a formative past intending to orient the present in service of the future that God will provide.[19] We gladly pray with Alexander Groves,

> O, send Thy Spirit, Lord, now unto me,
> To touch my eyes and make me see;
> Show me the truth concealed within Thy word,
> Find in Thy book revealed, I see Thee, Lord.

Reading Another's Mail

Would you do it? You find in your hands a special commercial offer wrongly delivered to our address. Should it be opened even though another's name is clearly on the front? Something in it might have value for you too. The vendor likely would be happy to sell to anyone. The name probably was picked randomly by a computer.

Dealing with mail has moral implications. Mail usually belongs solely to the one addressed, unless biblical material is in question. Much of the Final (New) Testament is addressed by name to someone other than modern readers. One book is addressed to the Hebrews and others to the Corinthians, Timothy, and Titus. The Gospel of Luke was written specifically for Theophilus.

A reader today faces the issue of handling someone's else's mail and deciding about appropriateness and relevance. Belief in biblical "inspiration" suggests that there is value for other readers. We are encouraged to open and read despite the name issue. The Spirit's voice crosses time, culture, and names. Knowing the original addressee, setting, and intent is crucial but not the conclusion of the matter.

One of the basics of modern Bible study is the task of approaching the biblical material in its original context, where it first belonged. "Meaning" is what the original author intended for the original recipient in that person's or church's given set of circumstances. Is there more? Indeed.

Placing a text within the context of the inspired whole of Scripture, as the church has done under God's guidance, creates an additional context different from the original one. A wise reader will take into account the original and the whole-Bible contexts of any verse or passage.

Recall Paul writing to the Corinthians. He mentions specifically that these believers have their names on the envelope of his letters. There's no question about that. Those names are significant but not everything. The apostle includes as intended recipients "and all those who in every place call on the name of our Lord Jesus Christ, both their Lord and ours" (1 Cor 1:2, 2 Cor 1:1). Therefore, good Bible reading and interpretation rests on two assumptions, one historical and one theological.

We must know to whom something was first addressed, the *historical* assumption. We also must realize that the biblical text, by divine intent, now is addressed to the present reader if that reader shares Jesus Christ as the Lord of life. That's the *theological* assumption. We now read the Bible properly if we are willing to inhabit its original world and then accept its message as our own in our world.

Here's the whole truth. "What separates us from the biblical text is not the strange world of the Bible as much as its unhandy, inconvenient claims on our lives. It's not the message of the Bible that requires transformation; it is we who require transformation."[20]

One now can read the Corinthian or Galatian correspondence of Paul and, as a disconnected observer, review the several problems of those early believers and the rather harsh suggested solutions of Paul. We then are reading someone else's mail. Biblical "inspiration," however, means more than that the biblical material is endorsed by God as priority mail fully insured because of its great importance to others. True divine inspiration also means that all materials gathered into the final collection of biblical writings have intentional significance for *the whole church of all time.*

The task of biblical interpretation is *not* reading another person's mail. We Bible readers today are doing more than recovering ancient meanings intended for someone else. We who believe are part of the people of God to whom the Bible also is addressed.

The decisive transformation that must take place is our very lives by means of God's Word written and as it is brought to continuing life by the Spirit of God.

When the Spirit speaks through a biblical text, the names and addresses of *all readers* are on the envelope. Problems faced and solutions offered are perennial, apart from the shifting of particulars. Truth remains truth across cultures and times. Reading the Bible properly requires opening ourselves to its world of grace, obedience, new life, and world mission. Knowing the original context of biblical writings is very helpful, of course, but not the only thing.

Whatever the particulars of yesterday, the original call of the Spirit through the biblical text is unchanged. It's an urgent invitation to share in the life of the Eternal, with all its demands and joys. To miss this invitation is to abort Bible reading at its very beginning. The Spirit and the Word are inseparable regardless of place or time.

Linked closely must be the individual believer and the community of faith. The Hebrew mindset was communal. The best Bible interpreters are those engaged in church communities that are reading and interpreting and listening to the Spirit's voice together. Understanding comes best when believers are gathered with Jesus in their midst.

Who can forgive seventy times seven? Who among today's fortunate will decide to liberally befriend the poor? How can the friends of Jesus manage to overcome the world without taking up arms? Who will respect the Earth, God's creation, from human greed? We should land on the biblical shores and begin reading, seeing our own names on every page of the inspired text. The reading should proceed through the eyes of the Spirit. As we become new in Jesus Christ, things will tend to become clearer and even possible.

There does exist one rare island of blessedness. It's where help is available for the ultimate needs of fallen humans. Here's a good description of this most special of places.

> When believers enter the sacred space of Scripture with a spirit of openness, deep calls to deep, and through engagement with the text, the human spirit reaches out to join with the divine. Spirit-Word joins with spirit-flesh. The Bible serves as a portal for this mystical union. As Spirit-Word, it opens the door, allowing the light from the future to stream into the present. We are home.[21]

These are beautiful words. May they become our present realities.

4

A SHIFTING EMPHASIS

Classic Bible stories often are now understood as mere fairy tales, if known at all. The legacy of recent thought has focused on the world understood to be operating only by "natural laws." These supposedly can be discovered, controlled, and directed for human good. However, a new vision of reality is in the wind. The Bible may be coming alive again.

The "Enlightenment" has shaped negatively much of modern thinking and even Bible reading. Its scientific preoccupation has enabled much human progress while introducing considerable loss. On the negative side, humans have been called out of the "enchanted garden" filled with divine mystery and wonder. They have been pushed into a more bureaucratic and secularized place where little room remains for awe-inspiring experiences of reality beyond the rational.[22]

Transactional or Transformational?

The recent discounting of the supernatural has had its Christian advocates. They have tried to reduce the Bible to a series of ancient words, ideas, and beliefs that can be researched, analyzed, and managed with our increasingly masterful scientific tools. The result has had its positive dimensions. Biblical "criticism" certainly has its place. The original meaning of a text in its original setting is foundational for any contemporary interpretation and application.

On the negative side, and a large side it is, there has been a general depersonalizing of the biblical text, reducing its reading to an academic affair of human activity. Specialized literary techniques have yielded fresh and sometimes more accurate readings. Largely left behind on occasion, however, has been the divine dimension of the biblical revelation. Little honored by some has been the present ministry of the Spirit of God in relation to the text and its fullest current understanding.

The overall result is that the Bible has tended to lose its ability to disrupt and reorient our wayward world.[23] The modern mindset encourages a backward focus on yesterday. "This creates a *transactional* religion more than a *transformational* spirituality."[24] A largely rational process rarely escapes the limited working of the brain.

Now there are welcome signs of a shift away from the negatives of this stranglehold of the "Enlightenment" enterprise Being freshly realized is that the Bible intends to be something more than a religious document for human analysis and discovery of whatever remaining good is found. Rediscovered must be Bible reading that has the potential of personal and societal transformation. Enter again the necessary ministry of the Spirit of God.

There are various ways of telling the truth. Jesus typically chose to tell little stories and speak in parables, means of communication least offering themselves to systematic theologies and final creedal statements. His concern wasn't so much rational transaction as transformational experience. Paul spoke against "fancy rhetoric" that reduces the message of the cross of Jesus to mere words. "The unspiritual self can't receive the gifts of God's Spirit. Spirit can be known only by spirit in open communion" (1 Cor 1:17-2:16).

The Enlightenment mentality dominating recent centuries has opened a "yawning wide and ugly broad ditch" between many Christian theologians and their personal relations to Bible reading. The world of the Bible jumps this ditch by insisting on a key understanding. "Natural laws" do not control all events. Sometimes they must yield to "miraculous" happenings since history is supervised by the providential government of God's constant presence and overwhelming power.[25]

Whatever its human dimensions, and they are real, the Bible presents itself as a living document of divine source like no other. It evidences throughout this divine dimension. Reading it correctly brings to the reader an awareness of the current presence and power of God, even direct participation with God in life as it now is.

Such a presently inspired reading of the previously inspired Bible requires adding to our human evaluative tools of literary analysis the large missing factor. It's recognition of our *reading Partner,* the current ministry of the Spirit of God who originally inspired the ancient biblical text. This Partner now seeks to assist Bible readers by illuminating the reports from yesterday so they are received as wisdom with contemporary relevance and transforming potential.

Recognizing this divine Presence during Bible reading brings the book of God alive again. This "enchanted" dimension returns readers to the original garden where Adam and Eve walked and conversed with God before their sin caused them to hide (Gen 3:8). God again walks with the faithful reader and life regains the possibility of change and joy.

Walking and reading with the Lord opens the reader to being "ravished with wonder by both the beauty and terror of the text, by

the shock and awe of a living God whose presence the Bible myste-
riously reveals."[26] That is both the reading goal and the means to it.

God, Forgive Our Tinkering

We now live in a reductionistic world with little patience for serious
reflection and concentrated listening. The Christian gospel gets
reduced to simplistic phrases, bumper stickers, a Twitter feed or
Instagram post. This trivialization about all things sacred mixes
with a shockingly short attention span now so common. Such a
combination can cripple the Bible reader who is trying to hear and
hoping to embody the Bible's message in the 21st century.[27]

Christians today must pray for God's patience as we face a
recent legacy of surface tinkering with the divine Word. Often the
tinkering has been motivated by the need to formulate "doctrines"
that we understand, prefer, and think are acceptably contemporary.
Many are anxious to teach exactly "what the Bible says." The problem is that we are less sure than ever about what that is.

One commentator mused this way. "Theology is the study of
God and God's ways. For all we know, dung beetles may study us
and our ways and call it 'humanology.' If so, we probably would
be more touched and amused than irritated. One hopes that God
feels likewise about us!"[28] Forming beliefs is as difficult as important. It relies heavily on how we read and use the sacred book in
the process.

Coming before the forming of church doctrines should be fall-
ing into a loving and life-changing relationship with the Bible's
prime subject, Jesus Christ. Rather than constant "objects" of our
scrutiny, Jesus and the book that reveals him seek to be "subjects"
who come to us from the revealing and transforming heart of God.
They and not we are to be in charge of the reading.

The last words the disciples heard from Jesus was that they should wait. They were not to launch their world mission until first they had remained in Jerusalem and were filled with the Spirit of Jesus (Acts 1). Missing the Spirit is to fail in understanding the Bible and engaging the mission of Jesus. The Bible is intended to be a living text that infuses its whole story into our individual human stories. This fusing brings to us the transformative presence and power of God and readiness for mission.

The Bible is the one book that comes from more than human hands. It's the result of the Spirit of God who once inspired (in-breathed) the text and now seeks to fill the reader with the present dynamic of that inspiration. Why? So that the Bible may come alive and be read and lived properly in any time.[29] Yesterday's divine *inspiration* seeks to move to today's *illumination*. Bible reading is to be a journey into the mysterious and marvelous current presence and mission of God.

The book of God must be gotten out of the hands of self-oriented "modernity" where it's been reduced to "an object to be bought, sold, analyzed, and unfortunately even used as a weapon."[30] The Bible is intended to be in the hands of every disciple who is open to the work of the Spirit and anxious to be about the mission of Christ today.

Brokenness Left and Right

A serious reduction of the Bible's current relevance has been characteristic of both Christian "liberalism" and "fundamentalism." Their means are quite different but the result much the same. Each in differing ways has reduced the biblical text to its "factual essence." When so reduced, supposedly it then can be handled and managed by us over-confident contemporary readers.

Liberalism went to the German universities for academic assistance in locating contemporary biblical relevance. Meanwhile, fundamentalism retreated to a defensive "inerrancy" stance that claims an errorless and fixed finality of the biblical text. This supposedly protects it from all contemporary perversions. Whatever the extreme, left or right, the sad result is much the same. The living voice of the Spirit tends to be silenced.

There is more to the divinely inspired biblical text than analyzing and managing and protecting its verbal particulars from the perversions of both unbelievers and misguided believers. The Bible is intended to analyze and manage and transform *us*, the readers. Here is one book where the tables are to be turned. The reader is not to be in charge of the text. Instead, the reader is to be read and changed through the reading and listening process.

The Bible too often is viewed as little more than a nostalgic and well-encased religious museum, hardly the explosive dynamic of an arriving divine kingdom. This museum mentality must change if the church is to have a meaningful future. The Bible's text and its intended divine voice too often are subtly silenced, impersonalized, twisted into propaganda or reduced to pieces of religious data for our brains. We quiet the divine voice behind the text, reducing the Bible to a mass of church words not widely understood even in the church.

If we contemporary believers can be freed from this artificial and arid reading trap, the Bible again can become mysterious, marvelous, and transformative. It can be released from being a mere historical artifact from respected times and places of long ago. It must be allowed to be itself, a living text from God seeking to take charge of us in the present on behalf of God's intended future.

The Bible comes to us from the mysterious land of Pentecost. It's the place of dramatic divine self-disclosure. The Bible is a document whose full reality goes well beyond its mere words. The larger reality is God seeking to be our God, allowing us to have life that pulsates with divine life and transformative power in our present time.

Ingesting and Being Ravished

There is in process a shifting emphasis for the good. In 1916 Christian theologian Karl Barth delivered an address later published as "The Strange New World within the Bible." It was the keynote for a fresh time in the Christian world. Barth insisted that we should open the Bible and allow ourselves to get caught off guard, be pulled into its reality and thereby changed by actual participation with God on God's terms.

Barth's setting was the disaster of World War I. The Bible had to be freed from mere religious idealism with its roots in the rationalistic Enlightenment mentality. The Bible is a distinctive book of God bringing a new world from above into a greatly troubled world below. Many other voices now have joined. They are calling for release of the biblical text from its rationalistic captivity, whether of the liberal or fundamental form.

The new call is not for a suspension of human reason, no simplistic returning to pre-scientific days. It's rather for reactivating the possibility of Bible readers again entering the wonder-full land of the trans-rational arena of God. Our scholarly tools, useful as they are, cannot exhaust what the Bible is and is intended to do.

One way to free the Bible from our human grasp is to "rebaptize" its text with more of the air of its own true transcendence. The Word and Spirit are inseparable. "No one has heard God's Word until he or she has received God *in his Spirit* to be the sovereign center of existence and the wellspring of life."[31] To read the

Bible otherwise is to read it blindly and head toward the wrong conclusions.

The biblical text is a "sacrament" of the sacred, something material that nonetheless conveys the non-material divine. When we encounter the Spirit in our reading, we become readers "ravished with wonder." We experience "the shock and awe" of a living God.[32]

The Bible's pages remain the vehicle of the divine presence seeking to transform each reader into an "icon" of that presence, that is, a person re-formed and increasingly reflective of the image of Jesus for the sake of others. Bible reading is intended to usher the reader into a divine encounter that produces evidence that one is becoming "holy as God is holy."

Such encounters are mysterious, possible, amazing, and much too uncommon. The biblical text says plainly that such is the intended goal in God's mind. "Christian holiness is not just about a *better* you but about a *new* you, new in the image of Christ as enabled by the Spirit."[33] We are to "eat" the Bible like we regularly ingest food for our stomachs. When ingesting the Spirit-Word, we readers experience divine infusion and soon find ourselves becoming holy, loving, and wise.[34]

Jesus said, "Take, eat!" (Matt 26:26). Eat what, a raft of right ideas, religious symbols, and proper creeds? Maybe, secondarily, but not primarily. The reference is to a person, *the Person* on his way to the cross and asking us to follow. Anyone who ingests him will never be the same again. Said Jesus, "I am the bread of life. This is the bread that comes down from heaven so that one may eat and not die" (Jn 6:48-50). Eat, savor, and be renewed in the image of Christ. Such eating is inspired Bible reading at its very best.

An angel once said this to John as he held a little scroll. "Take it and eat; it will be bitter in your stomach but sweet as honey in your mouth" (Rev 10:9). *Hagah* is the Hebrew for the kind of Bible reading that God encourages. In Psalm 1 it's translated "meditating" day and night on the divine Word. A more dramatic image is of a lion that has its prey down for dinner and can be heard growling, savoring, lusting over the kill bite by bite (Isa 31:4).

To really encounter God's Word is go beyond reviewing its words on the page. It goes to "tasting and seeing that the Lord is good!" (Ps 34:8). Ingest, savor, meditate, really meet the Master and be refreshed in his very image. Really read the old words and become the new you.

Reading the Word by the Spirit

There now is growing realization that too much reliance in recent generations has been on the assumptions and norms of the Enlightenment's rationalism.[35] The work of William J. Abraham has been one important step forward in a better balancing of Word and Spirit.[36] Spirit-less reading is wrong Bible reading, a dead-end activity. An "inerrancy" theory of the Bible's inspiration isn't helpful. It's based on a rationalism imposed from outside the Bible. We must not claim for the Bible what it does not claim for itself.

The Bible is the dynamic book *of the Spirit,* not one parading a perfected non-human literary prowess in composition.[37] Divine revelation is more the product of Person-to-person communication. It's less a mechanical manipulation of facts, words, grammar, and punctuations placed perfectly on published pages and stitched inside a black leather cover.

Perhaps the word that best describes the proper nature and authority of the Bible across church history is *sufficiency.* Note Paul's prayer when healing did not come to him as requested. Said God, "My grace is *sufficient* for you, for power is made perfect in weakness" (2 Cor 12:9). Christians should be satisfied with the

Bible that God has provided. With its literary complexity and human weaknesses comes the Spirit presence that enables a *full sufficiency* of the text for the intended purpose of our salvation.

The Bible's power has proven sufficient because the Spirit originally superintended the writers and editors (2 Pet 1:20-21) and now assures continuing sufficiency for all the spiritual needs of today. I say "spiritual" because, despite many "prophetic" voices, the Bible does not present itself as the last word on geography, geology, astronomy, science, or pending economic and military combatants currently in the headlines.

Overly arrogant modern interpreters search through the Bible's text for things of interest, sometimes finding what isn't there from God and using the findings for their own purposes. These supposed findings always require revision by the next generation of "prophets." God's Spirit continues to breathe through the biblical text for divine purpose, transforming believers into maturing and obedient disciples with mission relevance in the present.[38] That's where the sufficiency is and our reading focus should be.

The Bible does not provide a finished theology. Instead, it presents a sure path to the God about whom theology seeks to speak. It's more important "*Who*" one knows than "*what*" one thinks about various theological issues affirmed and often disputed among Christians. Jesus is the prime biblical subject. Being rightly related to him and his ongoing mission through his Spirit is the crucial matter. Truth lies deeply in the world of restored relationships.

Recall these words often sung by wise Bible-reading Christians. "Beyond the sacred page, I seek *Thee* Lord; My spirit pants for Thee, O *living Word*."[39] By divine revelation, God is "not so much giving us a deed to real estate as inviting us into his life. Revelation is God's personal 'I AM.' Christian truth expressing the 'I AM' is a mysterious relational web."[40] That marvelous web is truly the place of wonder beyond the potential of final scientific description.

Unseal the Sacred Book

Here's the situation. "The contemporary landscape is cluttered with the rubble of the Enlightenment experiment. The 'assured results' of modern scholarship are much less assured, and the time is ripe for fresh reflection. We live in a time with new possibilities. We are urged to loosen our grips on the tradition of modern biblical scholarship."[41]

The contemporary shift is a rethinking of biblical authority in light of its witness to itself. The shift acknowledges the need to deal with the biblical text *as it is*, not with the abstraction of a supposed ideal text (the "autographs") that God once created in perfection but never has chosen to give to the church across the centuries.

Recall First Corinthians 2:4. There is a certainty available that results from more than the wisdom of mere human words, even biblical ones. It's the wisdom born of the Spirit's direct witness to human hearts. How, then, can the modern reader gain genuine and relevant spiritual insights from current Bible reading?

It isn't easy! We must let go of one mindset and move toward the ancient Hebrew one. Jesus and his first disciples were Hebrew in how they thought, read, and believed. Such a mindset naturally permeates the Hebrew Bible. It can be read properly only with this in mind.[42]

We "moderns" have exercised too much intellectual analysis and neat categorizing. For too long we have brought this rational pattern to our Bible reading. We must no longer read to control, master, and draw from the biblical text what we judge best and still worthy. We must find reading power in Spirit presence.

Bible reading is to be more than human minds at work scrutinizing the biblical material. We must become willing to stand *within* and *under* the text, not over it as reading masters. Reading, teaching, and preaching the Bible should be done *passionately* and *relationally*. We are to be especially sensitive to its frequent language of poetry, paradox, metaphor, picture, parable, and story. These language forms are evocative and imaginative, not easily reduced to fixed creeds, strict laws, and ethical propositions.

The biblical God is not an abstract *object* to be analyzed by the logic of humans. God is a divine personality who creates and enters into loving relationships with us faulty humans who are to humbly welcome this amazing opportunity.

The ancient Hebrews heard about God mostly through storytelling, verbal recounting of the past acts of God with us and for us. Seldom were the people reading complex essays probing rationally God's will and ways. The Bible often shares its truths with paradoxes, leaving us caught between truths. We "moderns" tend to be highly impatient with seeming contradictions and ambiguities not yet resolved to some logical bottom line.[43]

Reality is logical, but not quite, not altogether. Divine truth often floats in such an unfinished atmosphere, not satisfying our calls for truth's precision. Christian believers are called to dare releasing their tight rational grip on the truth-seeking and proclaiming process. In favor of what? In favor of letting the Bible *read us*, instruct us, and then transform us. We will not have all answers neatly packaged, but neither will we need them that way.

To read the Bible *from the inside* is to open ourselves to the person about whom the Bible exists. The goal of the biblical revelation is enabling God to come alive in us.[44] Only then do we become able to see things from the inside, really see them. Staying outside invites a constant misreading of the sacred text, sophisticated as we may be.

Adequate biblical reading and interpretation must give attention to the place of *Spirit reality* behind the biblical text and in the Christian life. The Bible, even though divinely inspired, can be a dead book in the hands of contemporary readers. It also can come alive with an honoring of the present agency of the Spirit.

> Come, Holy Ghost, for moved by Thee,
> Thy prophets wrote and spoke;
> Unlock the truth, Thyself the key,
> Unseal the sacred book.[45]

5

THE JOURNEY
BEYOND WORDS

Words on a page can be revelations or obstacles. Language
is linear, selective, ambiguous, and culturally embedded.
Procedures for careful interpretation are required to
reach dependable meanings. The biblical reader must be on
a journey beyond the mere words of the biblical text to the
arena of the Spirit. Otherwise, limited understandings are
inevitable.[46]

n Shakespeare's classic *Julius Caesar*, Cicero speaks in Greek to
avoid a passerby from understanding him. Says Casca, "Those
that understood smiled at one another; but for mine own part, *it
was Greek to me*." This comment has entered English as anything
foreign and not understandable.

Much biblical language strikes people today as merely old
religious talk from ingrown and dying churches. What's heard
makes little sense even if spoken in the hearer's own language.
The meaning has been lost in the shifting of cultures and
lack of sensitivity to spiritual matters. Even to church people,

sacred biblical language can be so familiar that it's become cliché.

It's not what we look at but what we actually see, not what we hear but what we truly understand. The viewer, listener, or reader is conditioned by time and circumstance and even level of caring. Biblical meaning can go right over the heads of even "Christian" people as so much *Greek to me*. Meaning is more than the words themselves.

Authentic spiritual insight is a byproduct of the Spirit of God living and working within a believer. For the ancient Hebrews, "truth was not so much an idea to be contemplated as an experience to be lived, a deed to be done."[47] To really know requires being rightly related to the subject and willing to respond to the message.

Revelation from God consists "not in the transmission of propositions but in personal address by the Living God. It includes the communication of information, of course, yet only in the context of *mystical participation* in the spiritual reality that the propositions seek to express."[48] When reading the Bible, we understand only if we know its language and are participating in its revealed divine life. That's a tall order, especially for any casual reader in today's world.

Jesus said, "And this is eternal life, that they may know you, the only true God, and Jesus Christ whom you have sent" (Jn 17:3). Is anything obstructing our knowing this Jesus who is the perfect angle of vision for knowing God? Do we know how to read the Bible? Do we know the words but not their meanings? Can we see between the lines and hear more than the surface sounds?

Using the Correct Mirror

None of us can separate the influence of ourselves from our reading. We bring much of ourselves to the reading and understanding process. When we announce what a Bible text means, our own fingerprints are all over that understanding. "One of the most tragic effects of Bible reading can be that we read our lives into it in such a way that we find divine license for attitudes and practices that are *more base than biblical.*"[49]

The reading process is like a mirror. We look down into a deep well to see what's there. What we see, or think we see, often are our own faces reflecting off the water at the bottom. We decide that we are seeing what we already knew, expected to see, assumed all along, and are prepared to understand.

Matthew was a Jew committed to reversing the Jewish tendency of his time to see a wrong vision in its common reading of Scripture. Readers were seeing a coming Messiah who would be like what they wanted and were sure they needed. The Gospel of Matthew is saying to such Jews that the story of Jesus is indeed everywhere in their ancient writings, if only they knew how to read properly. Navel gazing is a common human fault, and certainly poor reading when it comes to the Bible.

Following his resurrection, Jesus went about adjusting reading mirrors. Once he was walking with two Jews on the road to Emmaus. They told the unrecognized stranger that they couldn't understand why Jesus had died, a tragedy denying that he really had been their Messiah. Jesus responded by freshly explaining their Scriptures to them in light of himself, not as reflections of themselves. Suddenly they came to really know this stranger and their own Scriptures.

Reading mirrors had shifted and the same biblical words in the Foundational Testament began reporting fresh meanings that soon would fill a Final Testament. Their understanding was improved when the face of Jesus began reflecting back at them from the well's bottom. Focus on Jesus caused the ancient words to begin revealing fresh meanings. Reading through the eyes of Jesus is perfect vision.

These two men on the road were sincere readers of the Jewish Scriptures. It's just that they hadn't been reading from the right angle and with the Spirit guidance. Jesus replaced their own reflections with the image of himself. He was saying to them and now to us, "Be with me, look with me, follow me, and finally you will really know how to read and live!"

I love the New Testament word *epiginōskō*. It's the Greek word for spiritual discernment. It's a combination of "to know" and the prefix *epi*. The prefix takes the reader beyond knowing superficially to knowing in depth. "There is only one means of discovering the true nature of Christianity. We must step out on this path, commit ourselves to its way of life, and then we shall begin to see for ourselves, really see."[50]

Recall the story of the man born blind (Jn 9). A deep irony radiates through this story. The people who should have been able to see turned out to be blind, while the one who actually was blind comes to full sight. Jesus was the intervening reading catalyst.

The Bible is intended to be a *transparency* revealing God and hardly an encyclopedia of religious information for human consumption and private use. Given the language, culture, timing, and other literary issues that complicate interpretation of all ancient documents, the Bible included, Christians should come to the biblical text in a particular way.

What way? It's the crucial journey *beyond words*. We should be looking less for what we think we can see and more being open to understanding deeply by encountering the God who radiates truth from among and beneath all the words. That's the move from knowing to *really knowing*.

Modern Bible readers must realize what should be happening in the reading process. The grace of God intends to be at work stimulating in us the image of Jesus Christ. As that image increasingly emerges, our eyes are better enabled to see the Father acting in the Son, resurrection life being present beyond sin and death, and eternal blessedness arriving beyond today's suffering and unanswered questions.

Is such a dramatic claim so much Greek to you? Look to Jesus for new life, new eyes enriched by his vision, and finally in-depth understanding. Read the Bible with this new mirror in place.

More than Skilled Wordsmiths

Bible reading is to be a life-changing process more than one of gathering religious information. It's to be a successful journeying into the mysterious land of Pentecost, the place beyond words where the Spirit is revealing the Son as our way to the Father, ourselves, and each other.

Encountering and participating in this divine-human process can happen when we intentionally open ourselves to God's intended insight and power. Pentecost is an occasion of knowledge stimulation. Pilgrims from many lands and languages had tongues enabled to spread the gospel beyond "it's all Greek to me." It was a time of knowing in depth and sharing with passion. It was true Christian understanding leading to successful Christian mission.

Eugene Peterson thought of his paraphrasing of the Bible (*The Message*) as a kind of *lectio divina*. That is, more than getting the biblical words right as a scholar and skilled wordsmith, his larger goal was to capture the vibrancy and livingness of the message. He sought to cultivate the reader's habit of *living the text*.

The ancient biblical text wants to become profound communication that exhibits and applies the good news of a loving and saving God coming to all people in all of life's circumstances. More than sacred words, this communication invites the reader on a journey beyond the words into life at its fullest.

There is no better time for the coming kingdom of God than *now* and no better place for it than *here*. Any self-centered Bible reading motivated by the blindness of personal agenda tends to dictate meaning more individual than actually biblical. Such reading is abusive and abortive. There was no timidity in Peterson's use of dramatic language as he paraphrased a significant comment of the biblical psalmist.

Peterson reports that "the poet was bold to imagine God swinging a pickaxe, digging ears in our granite blockheads so that we can hear, really hear what God speaks to us" (Ps 40:6).[51] Blockhead reading is botched reading. Have your ears been cleaned of all granite blockage so they can hear God's voice?

The Christian community would do well to stop insisting that believers read the Bible extensively and constantly without providing guidance on how to read it well. We need biblical hearing-aids and well-designed glasses. Recommended is a reading process that cultivates participatory attentiveness to the sacred text, guarding against reducing its message to a web of self-serving and impersonal definitions and dogmas of religious matters of current interest.[52]

Bible reading is to be a search for the actual presence of the Holy One who seeks to speak to the reader through the text for transformation and mission purposes. Reports the biographer of Peterson: "What mattered to so many of us who knew and loved Eugene was something none of us can really explain. You would just have to sit with the man, encounter his warmth, his welcome, the hospitality of his silence. You'd have to encounter *the way he knew God.*"[53] This way was a face-to-face knowing that should be sought by all readers as they open the sacred pages and begin to read, meditate, listen, and really learn.

The needed journey to Pentecost is a spiritual quest beyond the biblical words to the Spirit who is anxious to reveal divine meaning in depth and with force. We believers are tempted to do little more than long for the place where we can find the exact answers to our most difficult religious questions. Too often we claim that we've found them once we've done surface Bible reading.

Bible readers dare not presume that the Bible is the one inerrant place where God has catalogued all definitive revelations on all subjects of our present concern. Revelation is not that mechanical, never that impersonal, hardly under our control to that extent.

Algebra Doesn't Work

I loved studying algebra in high school but must admit that it's not an adequate language for Christian revelation. Its formulas are too fixed and precise for matters of the spirit. Biblical language always must be understood in context. The context is both the original historical and literary setting *and* the ongoing life of the text in relation to the Spirit. The Bible pulsates in new times and places with present divine life that is intended to guide it full understanding and current application.

Words in isolation have no dependable meaning. They gain specific meaning only from the way they are used in their contexts, even by the tone of voice, and especially by the gentle promptings of the Spirit. Every biblical text, especially when understood within the whole of God's revelation, shines with the loving face of God.

Spirit-less reading is faulty reading. Wise Bible readers must journey beyond the words. Much of the biblical material was orally transmitted long before it was written down. We are to hear these words in the context of the whole plot of the biblical story. Not to be done is making a line of the script a dependable witness to the script as a whole. Such perverted reading allows the Bible to say whatever the reader wishes.

Most words can mean several things depending how a sentence works in the context of the whole of biblical revelation. Language is ambiguous, especially when it employs the richness of symbol, poetry, paradox, parable, and metaphor, which the biblical text does very often.

If God had wanted to communicate with us in a perfect literary manner, through a perfectly preserved and printed text, absolutely fixed and fully clear for all times, it would have been better to have used the language of mathematics. It's much more precise than the fickleness of words. But how could God convincingly say to us "I love you" in algebra? Doctrines are hardly differential equations.

Instead, God has communicated fully in Jesus. He now is reported and interpreted in the Bible by the frail use of human language. It's best understood by personal relationship with the Spirit of God who originally inspired and now illumines the revealed Word. God desires that we live *in him*, understand *with him*, and has sent among us himself as the surest way to himself. That way is the person of the Son and the interpretive ministry of the Spirit of the Son. It's not algebra but it's all there!

This highly personal means of divine communication shows "what, in his heart of hearts, God is really like—indeed, what reality is really like. Our universe is a community of boundless love. Jesus offers himself as God's doorway into the life that is truly life."[54] God came to us as Person so that we as persons could understand and come home to God.

Any Bible reading is adequate only as it is focused on God and infused with the dynamic of God's ongoing life in the Son through the Spirit. We can see this clearly in the biblical story of Job. His counseling friends were sure that Job's troubles were self-inflicted, so they pressed him with their human explanations. Their well-intentioned thoughts, however, didn't reach high enough. They were wrong.

Job resisted these shortsighted explanations of his suffering. He knew his innocence and was certain that the real explanation had to lie somewhere beyond typical human thinking and reading of the situation.

Finally, Job turned upward and tried to put God on the spot, calling for some trans-rational knowledge, the higher explanation, the full and final truth. Asking for crumbs, Job soon got a response that was a whole loaf. God said, "Brace yourself Job because I now am going to question you" (38:3). Answers are found only in knowing the greatness of God and the great limitations of ourselves as readers of God.

Said the divine voice to Job, and now to us, approximately this. "What you need is not an explanation. You need to focus on encountering Me so that in our deepened relationship you no longer will think you have or need all the answers. Some answers are beyond your present reach. Seek my face, Job, taste my love, and be satisfied. Read with humility, aided by relationship with my Spirit" (Job 38-39).

Christmas Right Now!

Young Eugene Peterson entered seminary in New York City in the 1950s. He came from a Christian home, had a reverent respect for the Bible, but was tired of it being used either as ammunition for church factions in conflict or viewed as a sacred repository for endless religious rules, tired cliches, and sentimental slogans. Soon there was a seismic shift in his understanding of the Bible. It came in the classroom of Dr. Robert Traina.

This searching student was helped to retain a high view of the Bible while abandoning the view of it as an answer book that revolved around himself as the center. The Bible is not something to be *used* as a textbook of all assured details about God, a handbook of evangelistic methods, not even a weapon to defeat the devil or a pill that soothes depression as a divine antidepressant.

The new seminarian no longer was reading words in the Bible and deciding how best to use them as he chose. He was beginning a journey *beyond words*. Dr. Traina was introducing "inductive" principles of Bible reading that help take a reader inside the biblical text, making the text and not the reader the center of attention and current meaning.[55]

This inductive approach reflects Job's final admission to God. "I'm speechless, in awe, words fail me. I should never have opened my mouth. I've talked too much, way too much. I'm ready to shut up and listen" (Job 40:3-5, *The Message*). The biblical text is to be approached this way, with many more questions than preconceived answers.

Jesus Christ became the Son of Man so that we could become children of God. Christmas isn't merely a past event that we recall fondly each year. It's to be a present reality on which we gaze and by which we live. Granted, the divine incarnation was long ago. However, it's ongoing purpose is for a Bible reader right now. Jesus is born and now *is being born in us*.

We who read the Bible must do it in a way that patiently encounters the mystery of the ages and realizes that God is still reaching in love for us. Yesterday's incarnation in Jesus Christ is to be today's incarnation of his Spirit in us! The truth of biblical revelation always is more than can be read with human eyes and analyzed with human brains. Its core substance was born in a barn in Bethlehem.

The Bible's text carries an eternal "more." Job reached this goal, the more being the actual presence of the still-speaking God. He confessed to God that he "had heard of you by the hearing of the ear, but now mine eyes see you" (42:5).

The ears of the human heart and the eyes of the biblical reader always are to be attentive to this more, this sacred place beyond the biblical words. It's where one hears the voice of the One who is the presence of truth itself. Reflecting back to the "inductive" principles of biblical interpretation pioneered by Robert Traina and absorbed by Eugene Peterson . . .

> We read . . . . (*lectio*)
>
> under the eye of God . . . .(*meditatio*)
>
> until the heart is touched . . . . (*oratio*)
>
> and leaps to flame. . . . .(*contemplatio*)[56]

6

THE ORIENTING
BIBLE THEMES

While the Bible has many things to say, only a few are emphasized as critical teachings. God is and always will be, has called a people and come personally in Jesus Christ. The Spirit of Jesus is now reaching our way to renew, equip, and send on mission. The Bible is read best by focusing on these major themes.

Can you draw a theological map with one fixed point from which four lines spread out in all directions? If you can, you have the beginnings of being a good Christian theologian. The fixed point is the unchanging God of all times and all truths.[57] The four spreading lines are the truth streams that reach out from the very heart of God. Together, they clarify who God is, how God works, and who we can be as transformed human beings in this world and beyond.

How are we to read the Bible? We are to locate and recognize evolving elements of these truth streams that emerge from the one eternal Fountain. They are everywhere present in the sixty-six books of the Bible. They frame the many-faceted story of God with and for us and now seeking to be in and through us.

Current Bible readers are called to understand and live within these truth streams. They come together in one place, the person of Jesus Christ with his teachings now made alive and relevant through his Spirit. The Bible has one supreme subject, a proper knowledge of God from whose being flow these creating, cleansing, and guiding truth streams.

This is what should capture and guide our prime Bible reading attention. It provides a grace-full new life to those who read carefully and come to obedient believing. This life, once matured, forms one into an inspired image and worthy representative of our Lord Jesus.

The Supreme Bible Subject

Who is the *Theo* of Christian *theo*logy? The Apostles' Creed is organized around a divine Tri-Unity, one God known in triple complexity. The three-ness of the divine one-ness is the central substance of the biblical revelation and of all proper Bible understanding.

We read the Bible to find this God, who turns out to have been seeking us all the time! The Bible begins and ends with God, the great mystery, amazement, joy of all joys, the unreachable One who has chosen in love to reach toward us.

God is Self-revealing, especially in the life, teachings, death, and resurrection of Jesus, and now through the ongoing teaching ministry of his Spirit. The way to locate this central theme of the entire Bible is to focus on this triple complexity of the one God. As we read the Bible, God becomes known to us as . . .

Sovereign, the God who always stands and creates, the *source* of loving grace;

Savior, the God who stoops and saves, the Christ *initiative* of loving grace;

Spirit, the God who stays and sustains, the constant *presence* of loving grace.

These three are one and truly marvelous! Don't be puzzled or paralyzed by this paradox of numbers. God is always beyond our rational thoughts. Still, reports the Bible, God has come close and can be understood well enough to make our lives and destinies what they are intended to be.

GOD

SOVEREIGN **SPIRIT**

SAVIOR

A large question is explored throughout the Bible. If God is the source, initiative, and presence of loving grace, for whom is such graciousness intended and available? Who is included among the chosen people of God? Who is eligible to receive what God is lovingly prepared to give?

Biblical revelation speaks first of a select people whom God chooses as his own. Then, in Jesus Christ, this selection comes to be understood as anyone who chooses to accept the gracious, saving choice of God revealed fully in Jesus. God is one. This one is known best in Jesus, who was and is for *all people*, none excluded. A core biblical concept that defines the essential nature and intentions of God has been revealed as universal *loving grace.*[58]

As a contemporary Bible reader looks closely for pervasive teaching, discovered is the flowing from God of *four truth streams*. Together, they clarify from various angles the full intentions and provisions of God for all people. They appear in various ways throughout the Bible and always should hold the primary attention of careful readers.[59]

The Four Truth Streams

Bible reading should be an active searching for the God who is searching for us. The Bible reader should be seeking dependable truth and finding it in the combination of the four truth streams that flow throughout the text.

**CENTRAL TRUTH STREAMS
FLOWING FROM THE DIVINE FOUNTAIN**

COVENANT   HOLINESS   ORDERING   HOPE

The Way of *Covenant*, Stream #1. God is a seeker of covenant partners. God acts to choose a people of his own and give them a special mission. This choice is made out of love, not because of special deserving. The divine intent is the well-being of all people, with the chosen ones spearheading the sharing of good news that all need to hear.

God graciously chooses the unworthy as a means of reaching everyone with a saving message, which is most worthy indeed. The initial choice was Israel, then Jesus Christ who proved to be the true Israel, and now the church, the faithful people of Jesus. The church is the believing body who *in Christ* is called to reach out to all people on behalf of God's saving love.

The Way of *Holiness*, Stream #2. The mission of God's covenant people cannot be accomplished without church members being willing to be what God wants. The life of the chosen in all its dimensions is intended to be "holy" as God is holy. God's covenant people must be set apart, become like God, and participate in God's life in order to reflect God properly to others. The chosen need to be changed, "sanctified" for their own sake and that of their divine mission.[60]

The Foundational Testament reports the history of Israel in this regard, including its partial successes and numerous failures. The Final Testament highlights the actual coming of God in Jesus to demonstrate perfectly what ought to be, showing the way for the church now guided and empowered by the Spirit of Christ. Holiness, God-likeness, is essential for the mission success of God's covenant people. Without it the picture of God conveyed and the power of the witness will be seriously lacking.

The Way of *Ordering and Questioning*, Stream #3. There is a God-reflecting order and purpose built by God into the creation itself. Human life is to be lived in accord with this order and purpose. Because God's very nature is loving kindness, a key aspect of God's ordering was granting to humans freedom to choose whether they would live in tune with the very nature of things. To choose negatively is disordering, turning "live" around into "evil."

The Bible reports how the natural order has been disrupted badly by human choice, so much so that the original order now seems nearly invisible and virtually unreachable.

The mission and holiness of the chosen people of God sometimes encounter confusion, questions, doubts, and failures. The chosen always will be lacking in full understanding and only partial in their exhibiting of the holiness God desires. This limitation need not lead to despair. God is open to questions. God knows our human frailties and is patient with our failures in ordering our lives and that of the church. We are to live by the sustaining and enabling ministry of the Spirit of Jesus.

The Way of *Radical Hope*, Stream #4. God places in faithful covenant people a radical hope to sustain in the most difficult of circumstances. This hope transcends the fragile institutions of the faith and the aggressive enemies that oppose God's will and ways. One day God's Messiah would come, did come, and will come again! Hope always radiates from the Divine to the chosen. Here then are the truth streams in brief that culminate in hope.

Those in covenant with God (stream #1), those still in the process of being purified themselves by God (stream #2), those yet lacking understanding and still full of questions and doubts (stream #3) one day, nonetheless, will find vindication, fulfillment, and a joy everlasting (stream #4).

All truth already has been glimpsed in Jesus. One day love will prevail and justice will be done. Meanwhile, God's chosen people are to keep pursuing their mission, seeking their own sanctification. They are encouraged to ask their questions, face their doubts, and be stabilized by the hope resident in the Spirit's presence.

These four truth streams comprise the heart of biblical teaching. There is only one God and one truth. The truth has shined brightly in Jesus. It now is being continued and empowered by his Spirit and must be embodied in the world by his church. This is possible only as the church is able to embrace and share the truth streams. Meanwhile, God continues with the long-range plan of making all things new.

The Bible's Core Teachings

Jesus got his view of the heart of things down to two commands, love God and your neighbor as yourself. "These are the pegs; everything in God's Law and the Prophets hangs from them" (Matt 22:37-39, *The Message*). The prophet Micah earlier had gotten things down to three. What does God want? We are "to act justly and love mercy and walk humbly with our God" (6:8).

These two and three reflect the much earlier singular emphasis in the book of Joshua. When the land promised to God's people was first being occupied, the chosen people were warned by Joshua that their future hinged on one thing, covenant faithfulness to the God who was being so gracious to them.

Joshua rehearsed in detail the historical events through which God had brought the people to this pivotal moment of decision (chap. 24). Then came the bottom line of required action. "So now, fear God. Worship him in total commitment. Get rid of all the gods your ancestors worshiped on the far side of the River Euphrates and in Egypt. You, *worship God*" (Jos 24:14). That's the one big thing.

The future did not go well over the generations to come, leading to Psalms 105 and 106 where God's faithfulness and the people's waywardness are recounted. What were the people being called to do after their failures? The psalmist reduces the obligations of faithful disciples to four.

1. Repent!
2. Thank God!
3. Translate God's wonders into human music!
4. Keep eyes open for more of God's wondrous works!
   (kneel, praise, sing, and look ahead in faith)

Jesus tells a story that reflects the very danger of which Joshua had warned and the psalmist had recounted. It was about a vineyard's troubled history, faithless farmhands, and the danger of the whole place being cut down or handed over to someone else. "Stumble on this Stone," said Jesus about himself, "and get smashed!" (Matt 21:33-44).

We find in the Final Testament the dramatic speech of Stephen who recounts the history of God's people from the creation all the way to the crucifixion of Jesus. He blamed that on his hearers. This enraged them and led to his execution as a martyr (Acts 7:1-60). Whoever stumbles on the stone that God now has made the cornerstone, Jesus, will not survive.

Biblical revelation about God comes down to this. God is known functionally. That is, God acts and becomes known by the nature of these actions. Biblical thought about God comes primarily through reviewing divine activity. The Bible does not work with philosophic terms and theories exploring the subtleties of perfect divine being. God is *what God does*. The Bible has little interest in abstract subjects that Christian theologians have argued about for centuries, like God's supposed aseity, immutability, and impassibility. If you don't know these terms, never mind. Neither does the Bible.

Jesus showed no interest in such debates over philosophic nuances of divine being. Rather, he saw his Father creating, blessing, disciplining, and even suffering on behalf of the chosen and beloved people. The Bible's understanding of God grows out of awareness of this divine activity, culminating especially in the death and resurrection of Jesus. This awareness, so the writers and editors of the Bible believed, was inspired by God as *divine revelation*. According to Paul (2 Tim 3:16), all Scripture is "God-breathed and useful." While his reference was to what we call the "Old" (Foundational) Testament, Christians now broaden Paul's scope of reference to all sixty-six books that comprise the current Bible.

One writer summarizes the core teachings of the Foundational Testament by highlighting seven of its sentences.[61] They are orienting biblical teachings that support and repeat the four truth streams and the fresh faith expressed in the Final Testament. Here are the first two of the seven sentences.

Statement #1: Creation. "In the beginning God created the heavens and the earth . . ." (Gen 1:1). The Bible begins with God creating all things and ends with God creating all things new. This is the lens through which we should view all things in between. Where did they come from? Is there any purpose in life? Who are we as humans? What went so wrong? Is there any hope?

God was before anything else. Creation is essentially good, reflecting the good Creator. God is ultimate reality and *relational* in nature. God is intensely personal and lovingly *with* although not limited *to* humans and our world. God is Self-determining, Self-limiting, amazing love, voluntarily changing love's strategies toward us in response to our decisions and actions.

Statement #2: Abraham. "All peoples on earth will be blessed through you . . ." (Gen 12:3). Sin and evil will not have the last word. There is hope for humanity's ultimate future despite the interruption of sin. God makes a covenant, an offered partnership with select humans on behalf of evil's eventual destruction. Divine judgment and redemption are both real. Redemption will be accomplished even if the process requires much time and many setbacks because of sin's persistence.

With Abraham there begins a resolution of creation's disorientation that is recounted prior to Genesis 12. The process of resolution will continue until Revelation 22 is reached. Meanwhile, the prophets of Israel found themselves having to protest "in God's name against the perversion of the Word of God in the interests of sectarianism, nationalism, power, and politics."[62] God's people would choose to think and act too much "like the nations." These biblical reports are vital lessons for the church of today.

Jesus embodied the four truth streams and underlined the Creation and Abraham belief statements. A dramatic case in point is his parable of the "prodigal son." When read through the Hebrew eyes of Jesus who told the story, the central point is not about the younger or older brother. It's about the *amazing Father!*

In the Oriental world of that time, children were expected (required) to show the utmost respect for parents, especially the father. For the younger son of this family to ask for his share of the inheritance when the father was still alive was, in effect, to say to the father, "I wish you were dead! Treat me now like you were!" (Lk 15:11).

Jewish hearers of this little story would have been shocked at this request and wondered what the father would do to this awful child. The father, explained Jesus, at great personal sacrifice, gave, waited, and one day warmly welcomed home this terribly wayward son. Jesus was saying to his disciples, and now to us, that this is the biblical picture of his Father.

God is a gracious dispenser of undeserved grace. God is patient, Self-sacrificing, ever-loving and redeeming. God is Creator, Caller,

Redeemer, and finally in Jesus known as God with us on behalf of all people. Such is the very heart of biblical revelation. Read all the biblical pages on the lookout for at least hints of this divine heart. When found, repent and rejoice!

The Paths Now To Be Walked

We who believe must remain humble as we pursue our sanctification and the church's world mission. Theological truth comes more as proper paths to walk than detailed propositions to repeat. Streams are alive and move; motionless pools tend to stagnate and die. Biblical truth flows through Spirit streams.

Bible readers must recognize that divine revelation comes mostly in story form and Person-to-person communication. The primary streams of truth are teaching stories and narrations of events that flow through the Bible from God, the Fountain of truth. These streams are the heart of the biblical story and thus basics of Christian belief. The are found somewhere in all Bible reading.

The truth streams are more living rivers of pivotal meaning than fixed doctrinal statements and established church institutions. Doctrines develop secondarily as attempts to capture the meanings of the divine story. We must keep finding the Spirit in our reading of the Bible's story of redemption, thus allowing the Spirit find us. God's reading people become actors in God's ongoing drama.

Here's a brief glance at the central reading itinerary. The traveler goes from the beginnings of creation to experiencing slavery in Egypt; to the occupation of Canaan before facing exile in Babylon; being restored to the heights of Zion; being with Jesus in the wilderness before seeing him revealed on the mountain and murdered on the cross. We quickly wipe away the tears when standing shocked in front of his empty tomb and now are waiting for the trumpets to blow, the sky to open, and time to be no more.

We learn much from the long and complex story of God with us in Israel and Jesus and now as the church. We discover how God works in a fallen world by reviewing God's past actions in the many experiences of God's people among cultures and across centuries. We learn of God's intentions and ways and our roles among them as covenant people. Always, we are seeking our needed holiness, most proper order, and final answers as we hope for the future.

God is one and yet three. Truth is one, although arriving in four streams in numerous circumstances. One truth remains crucial as the Bible is read. Jesus did not die to change the Father's mind about us sinners. Unchanged is our deserved punishment for choosing sinful paths and the divine desire and ability to redeem. The Father is never blocked from forgiving our sin. The blockage has been us, our wayward wills and wilderness wanderings.

If God *is* and is *like* Jesus, then who does the Bible reveal that we are as sinners? Who does the book say we still can be by the power of the Spirit of Jesus? Answering these questions is what the Bible is all about. We are to read in search of the answers. They are there, wonderfully there.

7

THE WONDER OF IT ALL!

Were the whole realm of nature mine,
  That were a present far too small;
Love so amazing, so divine,
  Demands my soul, my life, my all.

—Isaac Watts

God rules the world with truth and grace,
  and makes the nations prove,
The glories of his righteousness
  and wonders of his love,
  and the wonders of his love.

—Psalm 98, adapted by Isaac Watts

Reading the Bible properly allows the reader to recognize and be changed by the sheer wonder of it all. A great Christian soul puts the emphasis "on the immediate awareness of relation with God, on direct and intimate consciousness of the Divine Presence. This is religion in its most acute, intense, and living stage."[63] The Bible draws a reader toward this immediacy and amazement.

Christianity is not a philosophical school for speculating about abstract religious concepts. The faith is more a communion with the living God in Jesus Christ through the ministry of his Spirit. It's truly amazing to realize that in this vast universe there is One who exists and chooses in love to come alongside and relate closely to us humans.

How grand is the majesty of God! How unmerited and yet freely available are the saving grace and power of God for us who are yet sinners. This is the stunning biblical message. Humans can approach the marvels of God, touching and never grasping. We read the Bible and come to know, but only in part. We become bold even while left with a deep humility.

If the reality and mystery of God were small and simple enough to be fully comprehended by humans, "then God would neither be great enough to be worshipped nor wonder-full enough to be adored."[64]

The Christian devotional classic *My Utmost for His Highest* stretches to the limit what we humans hope to do and be in light of the wonders of who God is.[65] The faith of Christians began when a band of depressed disciples got the shocking news that their murdered Master had just conquered death! They couldn't understand, only adore and trumpet the news.

We never will exhaust the mystery and the majesty of God. Even so, we are privileged to participate in the life-giving presence of this unimaginable vastness of love. Quality Bible reading leads to this gracious participation. There it is revealed that we can have restored relationship with the God who spoke the worlds into being and called Jesus from the grave. "Religion" of this kind begins at the acute, intense, and living stage before it moves to creeds, traditions, and institutions.

An Amazing Bible Word

Three Christian brothers witness to the acute, intense, and living stage of Christian faith. The beloved Christian song "Amazing Grace" is by John Newton. The dramatic story of its composition by this former slave trader illustrates the truly transforming work of God in a deeply fallen world. God causes unexpected and extravagant rejoicing.

Charles Wesley is possibly the most prolific Christian hymn writer of all time. A biography is subtitled *Man with the Dancing Heart*.[66] Two songs of his ask a question and express a deep longing. They are "And Can It Be?" and "O, For a Thousand Tongues to Sing!" Can God be that wonderful? Since God apparently is, how can I manage to praise God more and more?

The third brother is C. S. Lewis, a sophisticated atheist who titled his autobiography *Surprised by Joy*. The surprise was that finally he had been *overtaken by awe*. He explains the surprise. "A philosophical theorem (God) began to stir, heave, throw off its grave-clothes, and stand upright. It became a living presence. I gave in and admitted that God was God, and then I knelt and prayed."

When humans approach the infinite God, we get caught up in a sense of awe and astonishment. The Bible's call is to nothing less than "holiness." Somehow, it's for our becoming holy, *like God*. The will of God is our sanctification (1 Thess 4:3). How can that be? If it somehow can, our hearts should start dancing.

This puts us at the heart of biblical revelation and close to one amazing Bible word. What makes a person a "saint"? Sainthood is becoming overwhelmed with sheer amazement, caught up in joy, overtaken by awe, wishing we had ten thousand tongues to begin praising God.

This spiritual amazement is biblical extravagance. It's "excessive love, flagrant mercy, radical affection, exorbitant charity, immoderate faith, none of which is an achievement, a badge to be earned or a trophy to be sought. All these are secondary byproducts of the one thing that truly makes a saint. It's the *outrageous love of God*."[67] This divine love is a core feature of biblical revelation. It causes Christian believers to be witnesses instead of wallflowers, holy as God is holy.

When the transforming potential of love is unleashed, "people will notice, things will change, even the mundane will ignite with wonder."[68] The grand goal will have been reached, our *participation* in a loving relationship with God that enables our reflecting to others the very life of God.

The amazing Bible word is *hyperbolē*. It can mean an obvious exaggeration, a throwing well beyond, stating something so excessive that it's outside the ordinary, even beyond imagination, surely too good to be true. To read the Bible well is to discover those few things said to exceed human potential and even outpace our highest expectations.

In the writings of Paul we find a very few things said to have proven themselves so good that the best of exaggerations fails to reach the actual truth. These are the exceedingly extravagant things worth our full attention and excited sharing with the world. They are the great gems discovered by careful Bible reading.

Paul named them when writing to the believers in Ephesus (Eph 1:15-23). He tells them he had discovered a few things so outrageously wonderful that it was difficult to overstate them in human language. The divine *love*, *grace*, and *power* resident in Jesus Christ reach beyond all other events, persons, and truth claims encountered anywhere by struggling humanity.

THE DIVINE EXTRAVAGENCES
RESIDENT IN JESUS CHRIST

LOVE   GRACE   POWER

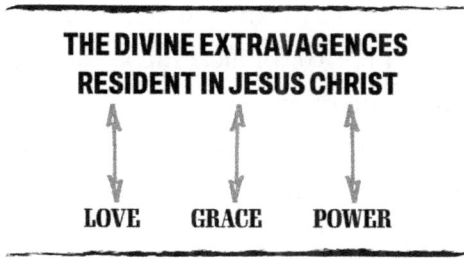

Divine Love. Humans long for true love and regularly display its common perversions in the public media. The love exhibited by Jesus Christ, especially on the cross, is a presentation of the true love that exceeds anything otherwise conceived by humans. It's the greatest story ever told. The cross is the amazing event that illustrates dramatically the extent to which God is prepared to go on our behalf, and with no deserving on our part. It reveals who God really is, sacrificing the Son, himself, for us. Amazing!

God reaches to the bottom of sin's disgrace and to the most unlovely and undeserving of humans. This love is without precedent and beyond all understanding, except as the Spirit of God opens our shocked eyes to glimpse in amazement. The biblical story is about God's acceptance of us fallen ones by a showering of love that can make all things new.

There is more. Jesus told his disciples that true love sometimes will lay down life for a friend (Jn 15:13). We sinners are said to be the friends of God despite ourselves, and God willingly has laid down his life for us! This exceedingly extravagant divine love is an expression of the very heart of God finally come in human form to help us understand.

Paul shares this dramatic truth so that we might "know the love of Christ that surpasses knowledge, so that we might be filled with all the fullness of God" (Eph 3:19). How can we possibly know a love that is beyond knowledge? "We know love by this, that he laid down his life for us—and we ought to lay down our lives for one another" (1 Jn 3:16). Biblical life is "having the same love, being in full accord and of one mind" (Phil 2:2).

Here are hyperbolic hymn words of Charles Wesley that should be on the lips of every Christian informed by a proper reading of the Bible:

> Love divine, all loves excelling,
>
> Joy of heaven, to earth come down;
>
> Fix in us Thy humble dwelling,
>
> All Thy faithful mercies crown.

The Bible centers in one key thing. Revealed in many persons, events, centuries, cultures, and finally in the coming of the Son of God (Heb 1:1-2), it's the awesome being and redeeming intention of the love of God.

Divine Grace. God has raised us up in Christ and seated us with him in heavenly places. Why? "So that in the ages to come God might show the immeasurable riches of his grace in kindness toward us in Christ Jesus" (Eph 2:7). Because of divine love, God has chosen to be exceedingly gracious toward us. This choice is grace without precedent and beyond full description.

We who are ravaged by guilt, fear, and inadequacy have been judged proper candidates for the wholly unmerited grace of God. We are granted opportunity to receive the forgiveness of our sins merely because of the richness of divine grace being lavished on us.

We are shown the mystery of God's will set forth in Christ (Eph 1:7-10). "Now may the Lord Jesus Christ and God our Father, who loved us and through grace gave us eternal comfort and good hope, comfort your hearts and strengthen them in every good work and word" (2 Thess 2:16-17).

How can God's grace be described? One Christian attempted with "marvelous, infinite, matchless grace, freely bestowed on all who believe."[69] Paul tried with "where sin increased, grace abounded all the more" (Rom 5:20). He told believers to "work out your own salvation with fear and trembling, for it is God who is at work in you for his good pleasure" (Phil 2:12-13). Any effort we put forth has a chance of success only because God's grace is at work. Wonderful! Amazing! True!

Divine Power. The way of God's working turns upside down the typical human view of power, putting it in an arena of marvel and mystery. The divine victory that overcomes the world of evil is pictured in Christ who reigns in victory even with the horror of an old rugged cross. God's weakness is stronger than any human strength (1 Cor 1:25). According to biblical revelation, God will accomplish all that has been promised despite any needed patience and suffering.

We see in the Bible God's power displayed by what we usually think of as powerlessness. Such odd displays are the working out of the power of God. Jesus, knowing who he was and what divine mission was his, tied a towel around his waist, knelt, and washed the dirty feet of his disciples. Heaven itself was on its knees. Power was in evidence in what appeared to be a scene of weakness.

The extraordinary power of God need not be displayed by the domination others, our human view of power, but by the empowerment of others for the sacrificial service of a long-suffering God. Paul speaks of the immeasurable greatness of God's power for those of us who believe, power seen especially in raising Jesus from the dead (Eph 1:19-22).

This miraculous raising, however, was not to destroy the Romans and Jewish leaders who had him hung but to encourage opportunity for their salvation. Christian faith forces a redefinition of power. God's power, while unlimited, is enveloped by a love and grace that frequently prompt its gentle expressions.

God is as Jesus was and did. This is the biblical story. Amazing! We are faced with a love beyond description, a grace beyond deserving, and a power beyond comparison. The Christian's extravagant message for the world is expressed well in these hymn lyrics:

> God's love has no limit,
> His grace has no measure,
> His power has no boundary known unto men;
> For out of his infinite riches in Jesus,
> He giveth and giveth and giveth again![70]

To be about God's business today, we first must read the Bible, be introduced by it to the unexpected Son, who in turn introduces us to the amazing Father. God becomes known as "holy, holy, holy," the One beyond us, different from us, working in ways not typical of us humans. Why this working? It's in preparation for us to participate in the divine life and mission. Extravagant!

Another Amazing Bible Word

What if it really did become possible for us to participate in the divine life? I don't mean ceasing to be fully human or becoming an actual part of God. I mean being restored to God's gracious intention for us in the original creation. Such a marvelous "redemption" is the key announcement of the entire Bible.

What the church of Jesus needs today is a membership that's participating in the life of this great God. None of us believers can represent God well until first we come into God's presence with awe and repentance and obedience. "Only then can we become *holy* by being filled by a radical amazement about the infinite love, grace, and power of God. Only then can we walk with a genuine difference because we have encountered the very different God and become very different persons."[71]

That kind of revolutionized life walking can come from Bible reading that hears the Spirit's voice and allows it to lead to Bible living! "Are you thirsty? The Spirit and the Bride say, 'Come!' All who will, come and drink, drink freely of the Water of Life!" (Rev 22:17). We should be amazed that we can know about God through Christ and participate in God's life through the Spirit.

Beyond being "saved" comes the additional biblical call to go on to being "sanctified." This means maturing in the renewed relationship to God in Christ through the Spirit. It enables a daily life that increasingly reflects the life of the Eternal One. The biblical announcement is, *we can be what we ought to be!*

This spiritual maturity is embedded in the meanings of another rich biblical word, *kosméō*. It means to adorn or make more attractive and comes into English as "cosmetic." It appeared in secular Greek literature describing an army marching in disciplined formation, uniforms perfect on soldiers obviously equipped for any necessary action. How does such a beautiful sight come about for Christian believers?

A famous violinist was carrying his precious instrument on the street when a passerby asked, "How do I get to Carnegie Hall?" The reply was, "Practice, practice, practice!" The same point is made by Jesus in his parable of the wise and foolish virgins. Christ could return at any time. One's lamp is always to be trimmed and in full working order. Believers in the Master are to be actively on the way to what they ought to be and can be by God's grace. We always are to be at the ready, practiced and prepared.

We who comprise the church are to be disciples standing in united formation, in obvious working order, in proper dress, well equipped, and concentrating on our duty and mission. This constant preparation requires spiritual discipline, focus, and maintenance. Our very bodies are to be living sacrifices of spiritual worship to the glory of God (Rom 12:1-2).

There is nothing attractive about a professed believer in Jesus who, instead of standing on the promises of God, mostly sits on the premises of the church. We are to model the Master, to imitate Christ in loving action, to be Spirit-related and Spirit-led. *Kosméō* calls us to be shining with the beauty of Christ.

The Final Testament speaks often of Christian "cosmetics." We are to be dressed in good works (1 Tim 2:9-10), building our reputations not with lovely perfumes and fancy clothes but gentle and quiet spirits that are precious in God's sight (1 Pet 3:4). An inner beauty expressing reverence for God is essential battle gear for the Christian. One must put on the new clothes that are the whole armor of God (Eph 6:13-17).

Our resulting witness should be attractive, "an ornament to the doctrine of God our Savior" (Titus 2:9-10). We should search the Bible constantly and listen to the Spirit carefully for the particulars of how best to evidence such divine beauty in our time and place. Constant caution is required because many life practices are only cultural expectations and not Christian mandates for all people in all settings. A way to judge, as one brother once said, is whether or not the result puts a "Holy Ghost shine on the face." That shine is ideal Christian make-up.

Jesus made clear that his disciples are to be lights to the world, shining examples of divine beauty that bring glory to God (Matt 5:14-16). We should pray as does this gospel chorus . . .

Let the beauty of Jesus be seen in me—
All of his wonderful passion and purity!
O Thou Spirit divine, all my nature refine,
Till the beauty of Jesus be seen in me.[72]

8

A SURPLUS OF MEANING

Highlighted with the Protestant commitment to *sola Scriptura* (Scripture alone) should be the necessary *testimonium Spiritus sancti* (testimony of the Spirit of God). Otherwise, the biblical text does not come alive as an informing means of grace for new readers in new times. The Bible often carries meaning beyond what the original human author intended or anticipated, while never in conflict with the teachings of Jesus.

The Bible is the written medium of the revelation of God fully expressed in *the Word*, Jesus Christ. It's more than its written words can convey unaided by the ongoing ministry of the Spirit of Jesus. The Bible is understood best in each present through that ongoing teaching ministry.

Under the strict guidance of the Spirit of God, the Bible and its meanings sometimes extend beyond themselves while always being rooted in themselves. This "surplus of meaning" is obvious in how the Bible is self-correcting and occasionally self-extending within its own text. There are numerous Final Testament examples of extensions and even alterations of Foundational Testament meanings.

There remains a biblical stability even with this flexibility. God is unchanging in nature and purposes, as is the Bible in its authority as sufficient for Christian belief in relation to its teaching purposes. The Bible's time and purpose of original composition is always to be respected, even if fuller revelation occasionally goes beyond it with the Spirit's guidance.

For adequate biblical reading and interpretation, attention must be given to the role of the Spirit's ongoing reality in Christian life. The revealed biblical text is authoritative, *foundational form*; the Spirit's ministry on behalf of the Bible's contemporary meaning is likewise crucial, *essential function*. The Spirit of God "both speaks through ancient Scripture *and* illumines the contemporary reader for real life and mission."[73] Biblical interpretation and expression are always unfinished tasks.

Foundational and Final

The Word of God provides proper perspective on revealed truth. For *sufficiency* in our time, however, it is be recognized that the Bible is dynamic in nature, only partially perceived by us, and more personal than propositional. The two biblical Testaments, one foundational and the other final, jointly reveal the Christ. Across their many pages is a growing presentation of the Christ who is the embodied Word itself. Clarifying the particulars of the ongoing embodiment of the Word in the church is now the work of the Spirit of Jesus.

The Bible developed over several centuries in numerous bits and pieces arising in very different circumstances. Its internal parts naturally reflect this diversity, making the result more an orchestra than a solo instrument. The full divine revelation does not appear all at once, possibly because humans aren't ever prepared to receive it all.

Nor is the complete meaning of divine revelation and its applications resident only in the ones realized in the past. "Surplus" exists. It's the Spirit's business to make such known in each new time and place. Truth is fixed and yet flexible in its understandings, expressions, and applications. The inspiring and interpreting ministry of the Spirit of God is seen in the Bible's composition, compilation, and now its contemporary readings and applications.

Jesus told his disciples that after his earthly presence there would be the teaching and empowering ministry of his Spirit. The Spirit would reveal and make possible more than they could yet even perceive (Jn 14:25-27). The Book of Acts details the pivotal role of the Spirit in empowering the apostles to continue Jesus' teaching and work (Acts 1:8). Such still goes on.

Given this developmental dynamic of truth's fullest perceptions, expressions, and applications, the Bible makes itself available to the Spirit for constant freshness. This dynamic dimension of the biblical text opens the door to human abuse of the original text. Responsible Bible interpretation is no automatic and easy task. Always present is a surplus of true biblical meaning and the possible entrance of misunderstandings from alien "spirit" sources.

A key fact must be clear. Proper biblical interpretation never involves establishing new meanings not fully congruent with the actual intent of the original biblical text when understood within the wholeness of biblical revelation. A biblical text does not mean just anything we might wish.

The goal of a modern Bible reader is to discover the original intent and then ask the Spirit of God to open the dimensions of its significance relevant for the present time. The Spirit is Jesus still with us continuing his teaching as he promised.[74] No developments of understanding are legitimate if contrary to the unchanging heart and intentions of God as made known in Jesus. Anything contradictory to them is not of the Spirit. Jesus is the unchanging Word of God. He is *the* way, truth, and life (Jn 14:6).

Reporting Without Teaching

With all its uniformity of thought about the most profound of matters, there also is in the biblical text expressions of a wide range of points of view. The Bible often *reports* things it does not *teach*. Occasionally it teaches something in one place that gets expressed more fully elsewhere. We must be careful that what is read in one place is not prematurely taken as final biblical teaching. A stray verse taken out of context is a common way of making the Bible say whatever the reader wishes.

Take the matter of women needing to be quiet in church and limited in their access to church leadership.[75] Cultural bias often has trumped biblical intent. The Final Testament witness concerning women in ministry must be understood within the Bible as a whole and not lifted from a verse or two taken from their larger contexts. In this case, the biblical whole is very open to anyone using all spiritual gifts given by God, be they preaching, teaching, or whatever.[76]

The Bible, when viewed as a whole, sometimes presents a range of voices that balance and counter-balance each other. Only taken together do they comprise the actual self-disclosure of God. Sufficiency is rarely found in the partial. Quality Bible reading requires considering the breadth of the whole biblical disclosure on any subject.

Some Bible readers aren't prepared to tolerate patiently such diversity and balancing. They insist that every text presents the Bible's meaning as a whole when such is not the case. The irony is that sometimes the most vocal Bible supporters are its poorest interpreters.

Humility before the written Word demands openness to the wholeness of the biblical text. It also invites reading partners of varying global cultures and theological traditions within the body of Christ. "To invite the Holy Spirit into the interpretive process is to deny our autonomy as readers of Scripture and to affirm our dependence on the Spirit and the community of God's people generated by the Spirit."[77]

We must prepare for a little apparent confusion and some hard questions as we study the Bible. "There is no way to predict what joyful discoveries as well as painful struggles we will experience. This is the way of our whole life with God. It is a journey with the Spirit."[78] We see this journey proceeding within the Bible itself.

Jesus redirected various biblical texts to reveal their deeper meanings (Matt 5:17). Matthew offers a fresh interpretation of Isaiah 7:14, one that the prophet Isaiah wouldn't have recognized. Readers are to be grounded in the biblical text *and* open to the Spirit's guidance in the potential surplus of its meanings. Such a surplus is hardly wrong just because it differs from the original reference. Jesus was Lord of the text and clearly not captive to the "traditions of the Elders" of his time. He sets the pattern for us.

The full and present meaning of a biblical text can exist only between the lines. "Sometimes the deeper meaning isn't visible until shined upon by the great Light that is Jesus."[79] Jesus didn't hesitate to contradict what was being claimed by others as fixed and unquestionable interpretation. Jesus had a short time on earth and said that he relies on his Spirit to now elaborate the fullest meanings of his teachings that his first disciples understood only partially at best.

The Bible often reaches back to its older materials and puts them in new contexts and to new uses, even with somewhat altered meanings. This process shows that there is room for the Spirit of God to continue updating the text. The updating is not *changing* it but more fully unfolding it and freshly *applying* it as new settings and situations keep arising. We believers are called to approach the Bible expectantly, listening to the Spirit as we read the text, hoping to find divine treasures that are very old and yet suddenly seem quite new.

Taken to excess, this fresh listening to the Spirit can work in a manner that violates the biblical text itself. Even so, we must not hesitate to remain open because the Bible often illustrates this process as legitimate and necessary. "Conservative" believers must recognize that Scripture always is anxious to understand what God is saying presently. It's very possible to fixate religious traditions (Pharisees) so that when the fullness finally comes (Jesus) it isn't recognized or accepted. The church can strangle the Bible with "We never thought of it that way and never will!"

The Text as Stable and Dynamic

The Spirit of God shares with the church and Bible readers of today a Jesus-defined liberty of biblical interpretation. The full meaning of a biblical passage is whatever God says it is, realizing that God speaks only unchanging truth. The truth is not dead but alive in the Spirit for each of us in each new moment. The biblical text is fixed *and* fluid, never changing and yet always moving. God never has been locked in any past, never trapped in any human words or institutions, religious or not. What always needs unlocked is our limited human understandings of the fullest revelation of God as the Spirit guides.

The Bible persistently looked forward to the fulfillment of the early promises to Abraham. The particulars of the understood meaning of these promises kept changing as the Bible unfolded. One day, Messiah would come. Would he be a conquering warrior to destroy Babylon, Rome, or whoever was exploiting the people of God? Yes, then no, and finally it was Jesus who did come, love, and sacrifice as the actual Messiah. He brought a new "kingdom" not of this world. It was fulfillment even if not one as previously understood.

The fullest of divine revelation pictured in Isaiah 53 was fulfilled in the person of Jesus in ways rarely anticipated. God's promise first came in a nutshell to Abraham and later was formalized in a covenant with a whole people through Moses. And then? There came the stages of the judges, monarchies, exile, return, more failures and false messiahs and then a diaspora spreading the people worldwide.

What was progressively unfolding was the larger picture of what God wants us to know of the divine nature and purposes of the people of God. Understandings played out variously over a long time, all being reported in the Bible with none taught exactly as humanly understood. The biblical text as stable and dynamic. I refer to the two biblical Testaments as *Foundational* and *Final*. The first makes the second understandable and the second clarifies what the first was pointing toward but hardly yet understanding.

The Lord himself repeatedly placed new constructions on old biblical texts, adapting them to the new situation of his presence as the fulfillment of divine revelation. The Bible, we might say, is not *flat*. It has contours that roll over numerous cultures with its waves continuing to wash ashore in our present day, now finally clarified by Jesus and being further clarified by the Spirit of Jesus.

The Bible is *closed* in that we can't add new material. It's *open* in that the Spirit of God hovers over the lines and words and continues to reach forward, illuminating the relevance of the biblical text in circumstances and times far removed from its original composition. "Leveling the text is disobedient to it as given by God. It's wrong to snatch a text from Scripture and pay no attention to the place where it was found or to other biblical texts that bear on the same matter."[80]

The ministry of the Spirit surely was present when the collection of materials was first chosen and placed together in what now is the Bible library. Once together, no longer can we consider Ruth, Jonah, Ecclesiastes, Luke, Ephesians, or Revelation as isolated writings with independent meanings. None can be interpreted fully without considering the others. We must recognize all the biblical material and explore how one part refines and enriches the others.

The biblical books are many and now, by the Spirit, they are one. The biblical text is historically grounded and yet has a surplus of meaning for our present understanding and application. The surplus always must fit the revelation of God in Jesus. After all, the ongoing ministry of the Spirit is being carried out by the Spirit *of Jesus*. Spirit and Son are one and do not contradict each other.

Every biblical text consists of both letter and spirit. Because we respect the text, we grant it the right to lay down the boundaries of its own immediate meaning. Because we are open to fresh meanings as may be implied in the biblical text or supplemented by other biblical texts, and thus intended by God, we continue to listen to the Spirit for these fuller meanings. "It is not enough to know the words of a biblical text; we also must know the *plentitude of meaning* that these words carry for the community of faith at that time and for our time."[81]

The church needs to understand its gospel message in fresh contexts, "not in ways that go beyond biblical revelation, but in ways that permeate it more profoundly."[82] Although the faith is delivered once and for all time, the church has not yet grasped its significance completely, nor will she until the end of time. We are on a long interpretive road and not yet at the end of the journey.

9

GUIDELINES OF INTERPRETATION

Many key guidelines of biblical interpretation are stated above. Central is the goal of the reader being read and formed into the image of Jesus Christ. Honoring the current ministry of the Spirit of God is crucial in this and other regards. Other guidelines now deserve attention.

The task of biblical interpretation must honor these four key assumptions.

1. Focus must be on the Bible that *we now possess*.

2. We must accept what we have for *what it intends to say*.

3. Then we must recognize that the Bible must be read with *the whole* of the inspired text taken into consideration.

4. Finally, *knowing and practicing* the faith are closely interrelated.

"Each step of a believer's obedience increases knowledge of Scripture's meaning that will be largely unknown apart from committed participation in the life that the Christian gospel requires and enables."[83]

Honoring the Bible We Have

The word "canon" refers to the fixed collection of materials that now comprise the commonly accepted Bible. The earliest generations of Christians received a range of documents about the new faith in Jesus and soon found that a particular set rang most true and were most helpful for the church's life. This set was formalized as the recognized Bible, the many Spirit-inspired pieces now being enfolded into one inspired library. To read this set of quite diverse materials properly, three things must be clear and accepted initially.

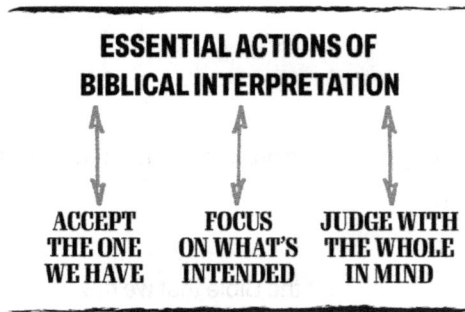

**ESSENTIAL ACTIONS OF
BIBLICAL INTERPRETATION**

| ACCEPT THE ONE WE HAVE | FOCUS ON WHAT'S INTENDED | JUDGE WITH THE WHOLE IN MIND |

Biblical writers and editors often lived in ancient cultures differing from each other and certainly from ours. Most tended to promote the dominance of males, the normality of human slavery and sometimes polygamy, tribalism, and holy wars. Anyone who has spent time reading the Bible has come across what seems to be teaching about these and other subjects that are contrary to the Jesus-inspired vision of Christian life today.

While the revelation of God eventually arrived to intervene, reflections of the world's views remained part of the push and pull on the persons seeking to understand the new thoughts and ways judged to be delivered from above. Even under divine inspiration, the biblical writers wrestled with contrasting assumptions that sometimes were still their own. We can see inside the Bible shades of remaining human thinking, different perspectives on the same subject that challenge each other although in the same collection of inspired materials.

This struggle shows modern readers changing thought moving in a more divinely enabled direction. When a biblical writer goes too far into one perspective (righteousness will yield a disciple's prosperity), another will push back and offer a different view of the matter (the righteous person sometimes will suffer). Such differences among the biblical texts have been called "redeeming contradictions."[84] One challenges and sheds brighter light on the part that's not yet the whole of God's intent.

Here's the critical interpretative guideline. One must not take a biblical reference to a subject and lift it out as alone reporting "what the Bible teaches." This piecemeal approach can be extremely misleading, causing the Bible to say whatever the reader wants it to say. Difficult subjects must be considered in the context of the *full canon* of the Bible. The whole often is more than any one of its various parts.

The Bible is inspired in its entirety, meaning that all of it has value in coming to understand the whole of a given subject that may appear variously. The contrasts on a subject should be viewed as having redeeming possibilities, we might say "progressive" revelation for pilgrims on the way.

There is a surplus of meaning which is not glimpsed all at once and everywhere. The Bible is full of self-corrections on its way to the fullness of truth. The more a reader grows into the fullness of Christ the better becomes the ability to recognize biblical self-corrections.

While the whole Bible is inspired, this doesn't imply that every passage is equally important in telling us directly how we should think and live. We come to understand the significance of various parts of the Bible by their relation to the Bible's entire story of salvation. The Bible appears less concerned with a particular *theory* of its own inspiration and more with telling us the *purpose* of inspiration. It's anxious to be read rightly.

Second Timothy, for instance, does not tell us exactly what it means for Scripture to be "God-breathed." Instead, it makes a clear statement of what Scripture does because it is God-breathed.[85] What does it do? It is sufficient in directing believers dependably in relation "to teaching and correction and training in righteousness" (2 Tim 3:16).

Two examples help. The Bible does not offer one clear perspective on the appropriateness of women leaders in church life. Rather, it states or implies a variety of perspectives, sometimes seeming to limit and other times depicting women as active leaders in different roles in different contexts. To lift one element from this variety and hold it up as the whole of Bible teaching is a violation of biblical authority and a misunderstanding of its inspiration. It's being intentionally blind to the whole of the subject and captive to whatever the current cultural bias or personal reference happens to be.

How is church life to be ordered? The Bible presents a long journey of God's people trying to sort out this complex subject. The ancient Jews lived in a world of kings and tribes and waring empires. At first they understood themselves to be God's people directly under divine authority and rule. Soon they were seeking to supplement this rule with an earthly king like their neighbors, thinking this necessary for survival. They got their kings and under many of them suffered and soon divided in civil war. Mixing religion and human government came with dangerous consequences. It still does.

We see ongoing development of this subject in the Final Testament. The people of God were longing for a Messiah-King who could free them from Roman occupation. Instead, they got Jesus who said his kingdom was not of this world. War was not in his heart. He relaunched God's people, but not as a church in the sense of a formalized new religious institution run by humans. Even so, like the kings of old Israel, soon there developed such an arrangement. The church of Jesus found itself designed much like the Roman Empire, the emperor now being a pope.

Ever since, the church has sought how best to understand and order itself. It has developed various patterns of church government, all claiming biblical roots. Jesus appears more interested in function than in the form of church life. The Final Testament seems clear. The Spirit of Jesus is to constitute, govern, gift, and send the church on mission, with the organizational issues fluid, not pre-determined.

The surplus of biblical meaning is what develops over time as the realization of the best alternative in given circumstances. Biblical reading inspires fresh understandings and organizational experimentations under the guidance of the Spirit. God calls, gifts, and sends as God chooses. God supports church order as seems best, sanctifying none forever and blessing all at appropriate points.

We who read the Bible and believe its core salvation message are being shaped by the Spirit into the image of Christ. We increasingly are in the sanctification process, that is, becoming obedient servants of the God who is on the move and never trapped in human categories, cultural biases, or social arrangements. Being freed to realize this is to be a matured Bible reader and wise disciple of Jesus.

Learning to Tell Time God's Way

Followers of Jesus are to be reading through the Bible, following the paths of his life and ministry, and celebrating annually his birth, death, and resurrection. Christian life involves learning how to mark time in a distinctly Christian way. This way is regulated by the past workings of God instead of by tracking the seasons of weather or looking at clocks and secular calendars for when to be at the next meeting, party, or parade.

We who believe in Jesus and read the Bible faithfully are to pace our work and school years, our vacations and holidays, the very rhythms of life itself around something other than holidays set by human governments. The "Christian Year" is a distinctive way of marking time as believers in Jesus.

This annual cycle of time measurement is a biblically set pattern of treasuring routinely the essential memories of the faith. It's a faith-controlled discipline that inspires spiritual growth by deepening awareness of core biblical teachings and how they should orchestrate the flow of a believer's life and that of the church.

The ancient Jews set the pace with annual pilgrimages to Jerusalem for the festivals of Passover, Pentecost, and Tabernacles. They would not allow themselves to forget the Exodus and Exile, who they were because of what God had done on their behalf. To be a classical Jew was to be intoxicated by faith in God. It was to live every moment in God's presence, regularly meditating on the Word of God so that life comes to be shaped by that Word.[86]

Each year Christians should direct life by the primary faith memories reported and celebrated in the Bible, especially those reported in the Final Testament. We should be baptized in the ongoing meanings of the Advent time of waiting and longing, the Christmas time of amazement over the divine arrival, the Lenten days of trial and sacrifice, the Easter springtime of new life and redemption, and certainly the Pentecost first-fruits time of divine gifting and mission.

We who believe must be shaped by these biblical memories and meanings. They are the rhythms of "sanctification" that make all of life an act of worship guided by the Spirit. Christian life should be an annual cycle celebrating the saving actions of God in our human history. It's the ongoing journey with the Spirit through our earthly days in anticipation of the day when time shall be no more.

Learning to tell time in biblical terms is the determination to do Bible reading and then living at their best. How? By living the Spirit life in every present moment in ways characterized by the past life, current image, and future mission of Jesus Christ.

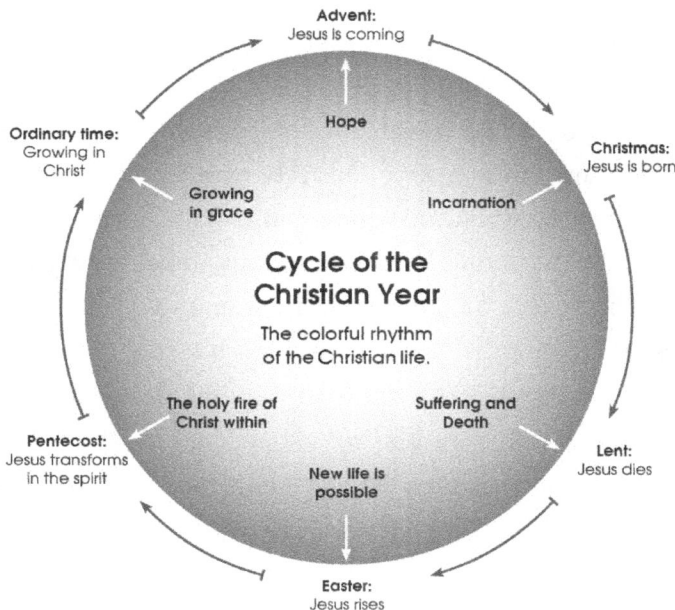

Advent:
Jesus is coming

Hope

Ordinary time:
Growing in
Christ

Christmas:
Jesus is born

Growing
in grace

Incarnation

**Cycle of the
Christian Year**

The colorful rhythm
of the Christian life.

The holy fire of
Christ within

Suffering and
Death

Pentecost:
Jesus transforms
in the spirit

New life is
possible

Lent:
Jesus dies

Easter:
Jesus rises

The primary goal of careful Bible reading and its quality interpretation is to enable two basic things. The reader is to *be read* by the Spirit and then *be formed* into the image of Jesus by the Spirit. A key biblical means of accomplishing these goals is teaching a reader how to tell time in God's special way and embody before others God's time being fulfilled.

The world is a master at teaching its kind of human time. It's time to get up. For what? Getting to work, paying taxes, answering all those texts, not missing appointments, shopping as much as possible, playing at every opportunity, squeezing out of each day the fun and profitable juice possible. From the biblical perspective, this is *chronos* time, being conscious of the clock's moving, being where we should be for accomplishing our long to-do lists.

Now for *kairos* time, the biblical way of marking time in God's special way. It's not the *flurry* but the *fullness* of time. Easter is the new time zone of God that calls us to reset human clocks. It's the launching day of God's kingdom arriving, Jesus being the first fruits and his followers the fresh kingdom fruit now to come on earth as it is in heaven.[87]

Hear again the *kairos* call to Abraham in Genesis. It's time to dare venturing into a new and unknown world. Imagine that moment when Moses heard God saying, "Go to Egypt and lead my people to freedom!" Is that summons somehow also for us? What of the pivotal time when Isaiah announced to discouraged captives in Babylon that a way home was suddenly opening across the desert? The awful exile was finally ending. It was a new time, a new world.

These are biblical, life-changing moments. God still calls to each serious Bible reader. "Get on my time schedule. Relax, repent, be renewed. Dare to venture forth with my promise. Accept the freedom and way home that I am offering. Join my people in waiting on my Spirit. Be one of those who realize that the Messiah *has come*. Live with courage and hope, knowing that tomorrow belongs to the Lord and today is your time of mission."

Time's up, time's full, time's starting over. Time may be nearing its end for any of us, maybe for the whole world. Time's not to be judged by what *I do* so much as by my regular recognition of what *God has done*. In Jesus, the kingdom of God has come near. We each must now live daily being conscious of this time-changing reality.

Marking time in God's special way allows the Spirit of Jesus to more easily pattern the times of our lives around those of Jesus. We are to be as conscious of the Spirit's voice speaking as our phones ringing. We are to become determined to invest our time and resources in the Spirit's current mission. When being truly Spirit-conscious, believers are in the proper posture for reading the Bible with depth understanding of its relevance for the moment at hand.

Chains Off, Eyes Open

The ministry of Jesus began along the Jordan River. I stood there myself one day. I was on its western bank just below the Sea of Galilee where the river begins its southward journey. I tried to imagine that fateful day when Jesus came to that same bank some miles to the south. I heard and watched a crowd of tourists anxious to be baptized in the sacred waters. Jesus did something like that long ago. His encounter with the preacher of his day was a *kairos* moment. He wasn't a tourist but a visitation of heaven.

John the Baptist was a powerful preacher loudly insisting that the arrival of God's kingdom was at hand and sinful people had to get ready immediately. Jesus quietly joined the crowd while John noticed that many Pharisees and Sadducees were present for some reason, likely spy reporters for the religious establishment threatened by all this speculative confusion. "Thunder in the desert! Prepare for God's arrival now!" (Matt 3:3).

John was pulling no punches. "Brood of snakes. What do you think you are doing slithering down here to the river?" He was barking aloud that a little water of baptism wouldn't help the filth on their snakeskins that should come off totally in complete repentance. Then John noticed Jesus and the tone of things changed dramatically. While Jesus didn't need baptism, John heard Jesus put everything in divine perspective.

Said Jesus, "God's kingdom is at hand! My being here is the beginning of putting together all that's been hoped for across the centuries! Baptize me, John." He reluctantly did and the sky seemed to open with a voice saying, "This is my Son, marked by my love, the delight of my life, and the future of yours!" (Matt 3:15-17). Time was being fulfilled. It had stopped in its tracks and somehow was starting over.

Here is where all inspired Bible reading begins, with this Person, these pivotal moments, this divine announcement, this stunning Spirit reality. When we open the book to read, we are at the Jordan River again with John and Jesus. The call is still to repent, listen for the voice with a grand announcement, and prepare to start life again.

When Christmas comes, the first thought is to be about the arrival of Jesus, not our needed shopping trips. When Easter comes, it's to be less about rabbits, eggs, and special clothes and more about divine sacrifice and amazing new life. We are to gaze annually at the cross of Jesus and be newly motivated by a springtime of sheer grace and sacrificial power soon to be seen in the empty tomb.

God's time goes on. Soon after Easter, we are to be overwhelmed by the Pentecost reality of being in Christ and, through his Spirit, sent to the world with dramatic good news. Eyes are opened and chains fall off. Can you read the Bible like this? The intent of Bible reading must go well beyond gathering information *about* God. It also must stretch the reader toward relation *to* and communion *with* God and then being on mission *for* God.

Bible reading is done best when it longs for the kingdom from above to come on earth as it is in heaven. When it does, fullness of life in the Spirit inspires a Bible reading that proceeds along a trail of regular amazement. It becomes a biblical journey of increasing understanding and growing adoration and deeper commitment.

The holy Christian-Year seasons are God's clock of the new life. They are central elements of the kingdom come and coming, signposts of the new reality that believers themselves are to be in this world. Christian time is about a time that reflects the victory of Jesus over evil. It's not merely victory time in heaven but current evil-overcoming time on earth. That's how disciples are to pray according to Jesus (Matt 6:9-13).[88]

The goal of time that's truly Christian is rooted in the dramatic prison event captured in a beloved Christian hymn.

> Long my imprisoned spirit lay
> Fast bound in sin and nature's night;
> Thine eye diffused a quick'ning ray,
> I woke, the dungeon flamed with light;
> My chains fell off, my heart was free,
> I rose, went forth, and followed Thee.[89]

When the chains of this world come off and our time is seen as now in God's hands, the surplus of biblical meaning begins to appear and life will have reached its intended pinnacle!

10

STANDING ON THREE LEGS

Three legs are required for any stool to be sturdy enough to sit on safely. When reading the Bible in a secure manner, there are three such interpretive "legs," often called a "quadrilateral." This word speaks of four but really means the Bible and its three necessary legs that join to assure the best of readings.[90]

Affirmed throughout these pages is the "Scripture Principle." The Bible is the primary and fully trustworthy location of Christian revelation that has come fully in Jesus Christ. It's the reliable medium for encountering and understanding sufficiently the God who seeks to transform readers into the image of Jesus Christ. The Bible never leads astray any reader who desires what this revelation intentionally teaches. The Bible is the "norming norm" in the proper understanding of Christian truth.

The Bible is rarely understood adequately by a simple reading of its text. Reading and intended understanding are reliant on three legs of available help. Divine "inspiration" means that the Spirit of God always is primary in directing the working of these supportive legs. With them the Bible stands as a sufficient "means of grace" for the reader. The Spirit carries on the teaching ministry of Jesus for life-giving and mission-sending.

An important caution arises. Such a Spirit-oriented stance to biblical reading and interpretation is open to abuse. How easy it is to misunderstand the voice of the Spirit, going our own way with private and unchecked readings of the Bible wrongly attributed to the Spirit. Such misunderstandings can be intentional or quite thoughtless. Regardless, they are all too common and must be checked by the interaction of the three legs and the wisdom of the reading community, the church.

Quality biblical interpretation stands on legs that enrich, stabilize, and help ensure a balanced and unbiased reading and understanding of the biblical text—to the degree that such is ever fully possible. Special attention must be given to the Bible-Spirit relationship. Said Jesus, "Let anyone who has an ear listen to what the Spirit is saying to the churches" (Rev 3:22).

The Sturdy Bible Stool

The necessary beginning is always accepting the "Scripture Principle." The Bible is fully trustworthy in regard to all that it intends to teach about God and human salvation. Its ancient text is the rare and wonderful place for a reader to land and sit safely in the chaos of the world's many truth claims. For this textual place to be sturdy, however, it is to be read in the most balanced, informed, and unbiased way possible. Its sufficiency is not automatic.

The supporting legs of interpretation form a fixed network of checks and balances. Each needs braced by the others so that jointly they yield the waiting wisdom available from Bible reading. If any one leg is not in service with the others, or the superintendency of the Spirit is not honored in the process, the reading outcome is questionable.

As Bible readers think, remember, and experience (the three legs), we also must know the inbreathing of the Spirit. This ensures the ability to read the many biblical lines with due regard to original wording and context and to contemporary understanding. Inevitably, we come to the biblical text with our own perspectives, biases, agendas, and limited knowledge of the ancient languages and cultures basic to the Bible's origins.

These combine to make a difficult reading challenge. Wise reading can't proceed in a vacuum. What have I previously experienced as true for me? What have other Christian readers thought? When doing my most careful thinking, where do I come out? What is the Spirit now saying to me and the church? The best available answers require all legs to be under the reading stool. They are . . .

Tradition, honoring the reading and remembering community, the church's long legacy of biblical interpretation. There's no need to reinvent the wheel. There's a body of gathered wisdom waiting to be considered and drawn on. In recent years, theologian Thomas Oden has made this point clear and provided extensive resources for accessing this gathered wisdom.[91]

Reason, testing for coherence of thought, the logic of claims, and the relatedness to all wisdom known otherwise. We believers must not park our brains at the church door but know that God's wisdom relates naturally to all other wisdom. The mission of a Christian school like Anderson University champions this vision. A published history of its mission is titled *Guide of Soul and Mind*.[92]

Experience, encountering and testing personally the impact of supposed revelation. Some things are known well only from the inside. Does my thinking work for me? Anslem said this centuries ago. "He who has not believed will not experience; and he who has not experienced will not understand. Knowledge that stems from experience outweighs knowledge derived through hearsay."

Imagine a baseball field. To score, a runner must safely touch all four bases, home plate being the fourth where actual scoring happens. Think of that final plate as the goal for touching the others, each intended to proceed ever closer to the scoring. The Christian's goal is to read the biblical text with maximum wisdom, having touched with care the tradition, reason, and experience bases on the field of interpretation, each necessary to reach home.

What have other believers thought? What makes sense in light of the best thinking? What is self-authenticating in the life as a believing reader? We must not read the sacred text disinterestedly, in isolation from our believing brothers and sisters, or with our brains unplugged. Reading should assume that the Spirit of God is at work in relation to all three legs of the supporting stool, inspiring our best understanding and current application.

Required of every serious Bible reader is more than mastery of technical tools for unpacking its historic roots. Reading is to be done in a "relational mode," prayerfully, obediently, in conversation with the church of yesterday, and considering all knowledge from any source. Care must be taken since claimed "knowledge" often deserves being questioned for accuracy.

Feel-good religion can be satisfying and yet wrong. Thoughtless religion can be welcomed because it demands little of us and thereby also be wrong. Without memory of and appreciation for the Christian past, Bible reading may save time and also be walking blindly. Wisdom lies in the discipline of wholeness. Read, remember, and think, being open to experiencing the quiet speaking of the Spirit of God. Ideally, do all this in conversation with fellow believers who also are reading the text and seeking God's wisdom.

Reflecting on the Quad

Each Bible interpreter, whether an individual, church body, or faith tradition, tends to prioritize the three legs of the stool. One leg is judged most appropriate and useful and allowed to dominate the process. We all are guilty of prioritizing, consciously or not, and needing the balancing correction of our sisters and brothers in the faith.

William J. Abraham first read John Wesley because he was trying to get his intellectual bearings "for my tangled and confusing spiritual journey." Billy was impressed by John's clarity, forthrightness, and honesty, and how versatile he was theologically and philosophically. Even so, the following tradition of Wesley (Methodism) often is thought of as "long on experience and short on reflection."[93] This presumed excessive length reflects the influence of Pietism on Wesley. It tends to be long on Christian experience and a bit short otherwise.

John B. Cobb had experienced a major crisis of faith and launched a personal quest for spiritual recovery. His was a theological reconstruction driven by a dominating consciousness of the modern setting and his requiring a faith that he judged relevant and rationally defensible. John found it with the guidance of the "process" philosophy of Alfred North Whitehead. This seemed to fit well the modern culture's preoccupation with a fluid *becoming* rather than the more static *being*. "I am a liberal who has tried to free Christian theology from its unbiblical views of God."[94]

Thoms C. Oden went the other way. He experienced a dramatic shift from being a modern "liberal" to a vigorous champion of "classical" Christianity. He challenged many aspects of the "modernism" that once he had embraced. This new path included pursuing the depths of the Christian spiritual life following the ancient pattern of the Benedictines.[95] Spiritual experience was prioritized over a rationality focused on seeking modern relevance.

Roger E. Olson has a Pentecostal and Pietistic background. Never leaving a Christian conservatism with its basic belief about God in Christ through the Spirit, he did leave the aspects of his background that came to be judged excessively emotional and anti-intellectual. "We all live the stories that frame our perceived identities and truth perceptions. We are to be open to the ongoing work of the Spirit in our search for the fuller truth and its best contemporary expressions and applications."[96]

Christian theologians like these and so many others necessarily address all legs of the interpretive stool that enables the best understanding of biblical revelation. However, they value and relate the three legs somewhat differently and with rather different outcomes. All Bible readers and interpreters face this sobering conclusion of Malcolm Muggeridge:

> Civilizations come and go, leaving their debris behind for archaeologists to dig through and diagnose—philosophers who are credible and then scorned; today's beliefs, tomorrow's folly; today's hero, tomorrow's villain; Towers of Babel everlastingly being built and never finished.[97]

This picture of human truth seeking is humbling and brings us back to the crucial ministry of the Spirit of God. All Bible readers are travelers on a continuing faith journey. Here's the good news. The God who calls us to this journey walks by our side, promising to show us the way. There is forgiveness if we do not see the way clearly or follow it most wisely. Never are we alone.

We believing Bible readers seek to think our best thoughts. We hope to honor and profit from the great cloud of witnesses who have gone before. We realize that we are called to get in the game, put ourselves on the line, reach out and risk in faith.

Reading wisdom then comes from the combination of these reading actions, all under the Spirit's supervision. We must keep reading the good book, not thoughtlessly, never in isolation or impersonally. Beyond information, the search is for personal and church transformation and mission.

Good Christian Grammar

The Christian Bible reader should determine to be warmly convictional without being coldly creedal. Good reading gives substance to faith without achieving full perfection. A "fundamentalist" tends to go too far, removing both the "fun" and "mental" from the equation. Left is mostly a pre-set and mandatory compliance with truth as supposedly known for sure as propositionally stated. They insist that nothing can be otherwise and resist anyone further testing what each leg of the stool may have to offer that could lead another way.

In the name of defending the integrity of the faith, some zealous believers overreact and compromise the faith by their own extremes. Using grammar to state this, readers should go easy on the expletives and typically pair fixed nouns with dynamic verbs. Christians should resist a constant use of final periods and recognize the ongoing value of commas. For instance, "we are saved," (comma) and still working out our salvation. The faith journey is not complete. Periods often give the wrong impression.

We Bible readers are cautioned to be sparse in the use of exclamation points. Such tends to announce dramatic conclusions not to be questioned and supposedly determine the correct approach to many other things. Exceptions are "God is!" and "Jesus is risen!" and "The Spirit still speaks!" Good theology features cautious grammar. Only an occasional Bible verse deserves to be seen in all capital letters.

The Bible includes an interesting combination of tenses. God's future is *now*.[98] In many ways, yesterday is still present today and the still-coming future has arrived. There is a Greek tense often encountered in the Final Testament that speaks of something done in the past that continues in its completed state. The door was opened yesterday and, by implication, is still standing open. Other things in the past are done and must be redone repeatedly. Believing is a daily business.

The God who was in Jesus always had been in him and always will be. God has come in Jesus and that coming is still very active in its continued coming of the Spirit. The devil continues to have power although already is decisively defeated.

The kingdom of God yet to come already is here! This exclamation point is deliberate since this reality is so wonderful and makes so much possible in the present. Good Bible reading requires quality grammar usage. Much theology is quietly buried in the mechanics of subtle language. Get out your commas and keep going!

Remember the beloved *Peanuts* comic strip? Linus once announced this to a disinterested Charlie Brown. "The way I see it, the cow jumping over the Moon indicates a rise in farm prices. That part about the dish running away with the spoon must refer to the consumer." Linus stops and insists that Charlie announce whether he agrees. Charlie walks away mumbling something theologically significant. "I don't pretend to be a student of prophetic literature!"

Few of us are such students, although many announce with powerful conviction their theories, end-time schemes, and "what the Bible says" proclamations. They sit dangerously on the Bible's interpretation stool with only one or two supporting legs under it. How much better to begin with a long-considered theological basic like this. "It wasn't the nails that held Jesus to the cross but the sacrificing and profound love of the Father!" That announcement deserves the exclamation point. It has been probed by the best thinking and believed across the centuries. It has transformed lives by the hundreds of millions.

All Christian theologies are written somewhere other than in heaven. If good, they are filled with the heaven that already has come in the person of Jesus and understood best through the wisdom of his Spirit based solidly in biblical revelation. Christian theology must radiate the special grammar of saving grace. The Bible is fully trustworthy and sufficient if read confidently, expectantly, and yet carefully.

The Elements of Quality Reading

How does a believer read best the Bible? There are many inter-pretive tools, contexts, theological traditions, and cultural nuances that lie behind the original writing and challenge current reading. There is no reader manual explaining the five sure steps to reading perfection. What can the church do to train modern disciples to read with care? The answer must go beyond any reading *method*, even if some are clearly better than others.

The best available answer probably is to change the question. Here is the better question. What can the church do to encourage the development of spiritually mature disciples who are anxious and well prepared to read the Bible *through the eyes of the Spirit*. Possession of the right reading tools is important indeed, but never enough. Approaching the Bible dispassionately, objectively, and only technically is a hurtful holdover of the Enlightenment mind-set that's now in serious question.

The better approach is the humble search for being mastered by the Bible's message rather than trying to master the bulk of its religious data. Here are two superb preparation steps for gain-ing the ability to read the Bible well. As a maturing believer and humble reader, be transformed into the image of Jesus Christ and listen with care to the voice of the Spirit in serious conversation with believing sisters and brothers.

Recall the *four truth streams* of the Bible's teaching and the *three legs* on which biblical interpretation stands. They join to provide proper focus if not full consensus on the bottom lines of difficult issues. Recall that biblical authority isn't located in any one verse taken from its original context. The Bible's authority isn't found in a solo announcement but within the orchestra of biblical voices on the subject at hand.

Remember that there is a possible "surplus" of meaning not totally clear within the Bible itself but increasingly evident as the Spirit of Jesus ministers biblical truth in new times and places, now with new questions raised and presumed information available. What does this newness imply when not directly addressed biblically?

Our surrounding culture, now mostly not accepting biblical authority, has its say and can be very influential on how Christians currently think. What can we learn from Jesus directly or by implication? We must avoid allowing our personal preferences or immediate cultural biases to dominate.

One Christian blog site is intended for "irenic exploration and conversation." That intention is a good start to careful Bible reading. Our Bible reading should allow listening to and loving each other as believers, with none acting like God. Believers must learn to read with care, listen with care, and love extensively when the bottom lines remain inconsistent in the judgments of the church.

Bible reading requires ongoing patience and humility. Is the outcome of someone's reading motivated by selfishness or righteousness? Is Jesus being honored in the process of biblical discovery and implementation? Is there obvious evidence of having seriously listened to the Spirit of God? Are we Bible readers able to reach lovingly to each other even when in honest disagreement, or has legalism and arrogance stiffened our necks and divided the witness of Christ in this world?

The challenge has been there always. In the earliest church there was sharp disagreement about whether salvation in Christ was available to a non-Jew without that person first accepting Judaism. Struggling with that painful question radiates throughout several books of the Final Testament. One view finally became accepted widely, but not without difficulty and the passing of time.

Love and patience are to prevail in the church as the work goes on to understand best the full import of God's revelation in new times and circumstances. Current cultural and scientific thinking is to be taken seriously, of course, although not necessarily baptized as assured Christian teaching. The wisdom of a respected Quaker brother is worth keeping in mind.

"Reliance on the ancient authorities for the very meaning of Christianity is not being blindly anchored to some outdated yesterday. There is nothing more forward-looking than taking the risk of allowing ourselves to be addressed by the texts of the Bible and the best of well-tested tradition, especially if we think hard and well in the process."[99]

Such guidance is the interpretive action of the biblical stool when all three of its supporting legs are engaged. Each is to be honored with none dominating.

11

SEEING WHAT IS THERE

To see a world in a grain of sand,

and a heaven in a wild flower;

Hold infinity in the palm of your hand,

and eternity in an hour.

The only victory is in Jesus, the man who died, and the only hope for the future lies in his triumph over death. There never can be any other victory or any other hope.

The above are the insightful words of Malcolm Muggeridge as he reflects on poetic lines of the English poet William Blake.[100] It was in the wake of World War II and the rediscovery by Muggeridge of the eternal significance of the cross and resurrection of Jesus. Those were the hours in which eternity appeared, infinity was held in the palm of history's hand, and a new world was seen in a grain of sand.

When we humans gaze at life with its many conflicting events and interpretations, often we don't see what's there. Have you ever held infinity in your hand by holding close a newborn child? Bible reading can make such a marvel come close and be read properly.

Quality Bible reading must go well beyond a casual skimming of the many words and a technical addressing of the numerous questions about the ancient text. It must center in why we come to read in the first place. We are to come seeking infinity in the fleeting present and divinity in the distant past. We come as broken sinners needing new life by the sheer grace of God. It's found in an unlikely place, the story of life from death on a cruel cross long ago.

Biblical authority lies in believing that the Bible is indeed God's Word written, divine communication sufficient for our needs. God's revelation can't be cornered in mere words and yet is found in a book. Its pages reveal dependably the nature and ways of God in human history for the sake of human salvation. It's sufficient to show us what we really need to see.

The wise Bible reader will read the text being open to the Spirit's ministry of shaping humble souls ever more closely to the image of Jesus Christ. The Spirit of God is waiting. God is inviting our coming to the Bible with this personal transformation goal in mind. We might not find all the answers to our many literary, theological, scientific, and ethical questions. What we will find is the gracious life of God flooding into and then out through our lives.

Once having received the privilege of participating in such life from above, it becomes easier for a believer to live comfortably without all questions yet answered or victories won. We will have been given a gracious glimpse of the real context and eventual destiny of all things. That should be enough. For that vision we should read.

Get Lost and Found

Vincent Van Gogh, nineteenth century Dutch painter, presents one picture of human life. Despite creating famous paintings of sunflowers and starry nights, he was overtaken by insanity and committed suicide at age thirty-seven. He wrote this just before the end. "I feel a failure. This is my destiny that I accept." Reality, however, isn't necessarily what is there but what is seen as apparently there. Whatever our present life circumstance, we are called to pick up the Bible, read, and live.

As we read, we are to remember who is the Master of the biblical text and discover that it's *not the reader*. Assisted by the guidelines above, the reader is to come into relationship with the one God who is also three. From among the four truth streams and making use of the three legs of responsible biblical interpretation, the reader becomes aware of and is changed by the three divine extravagances. Looking beyond the biblical words for the voice of the Spirit, the reader learns to tell God's time, become willing to use good theological grammar, and read someone's else's mail for the "surplus" that's likely meant for the current reader.

As the Bible is read, there is to be regular awareness of the guidance given by Paul to the Ephesians. "You were dead" (2:1) and now have been "raised up with him" (2:6) and are "alive together with Christ" (2:5). Resurrection defines the life of Jesus and now our own in him. We were sin-dead; now we are resurrection-alive. Being alive in Christ, our Bible reading ability sharpens. We are better able to see what is really there.

It's inevitable that we all carry into Christian life and Bible reading old cemetery assumptions and habits from the old life. We require ongoing reorientation as we seek to mature into the "full stature of Christ" (4:13). Bible reading challenges the old assumptions and habits as it reports the resurrection of Jesus and lights the path to our increasing spiritual maturity and reading sharpness. Relationship to Jesus through the Spirit interprets the resurrection and empowers the light by which we read and live.

The Bible intends to show us what's really there, granting divine perspective on the trials and questions of daily life. There are the flowers and starry skies of God's eternal love and new life. Van Gogh painted images of them but in his despair failed to really see. Such beauty is both there and reaching our way! Read the biblical revelation and see ever more deeply. Get lost in the biblical story and, in that very lostness, finally be found!

We are to allow the story of biblical revelation to become our story, its view of ultimate reality the lens through which we look at ourselves, those around us, and the future yet to come. The Bible story exposes the drama of the world's reality, the sin-salvation plot going on, and its only viable resolution at the end of day.

Read this greatest of all stories. Dare to let it *read you* and change you by the Spirit into the image of Jesus Christ. Our human destiny can be a gracious redemption by the sheer love of the redeeming God. The Bible's sufficiency is more than adequate to make this clear.

Dangerous Snake to Morning Star

Proper Bible reading brings one to where fear and light collide. The reader must stops forever trying to analyze the text and begin to allow the text to analyze the reader. When we've really come to the Bible, we will have allowed it to come to us. All along, the Spirit of God has been seeking us through the inspiration of the divine Word written, calling us upward to our new selves in the image of Jesus Christ.

There's a little story about a living death that destroys life. A man was condemned to spend a night in a small cell of total darkness, warned that in one corner was a deadly snake. If he called the snake's attention to himself in any way, life suddenly would be over.

So, all night, in the silent darkness, the terrified man stayed stiffly in his corner, trying not to move a muscle or make any sound, even with his breathing.

Finally, the light of morning slipped into the cell with a dramatic revelation. In the corner opposite the helpless man was nothing but a piece of old rope. The moral? In many of the rooms of our human minds and memories there are old ropes that have us virtually dead in our private darkness. Fear holds us prisoner while we wait for the invasion of any light that might reveal a better truth.

The Bible carries invading light and the best truth of all. Another snake story is found in Genesis 3:1. It launches the plot of the whole Bible. Fear and darkness cripple humanity, freezing us in our little cell corners. There is desperate need for the morning light of divine redemption. The fearsome snake, while very troubling, turns out to already be reduced to a mere rope--if we only knew it and dared to act like it were so.

Let's read the Bible to see what's really there in the corners our troubled lives. Present is no longer a dangerous snake but a lovely Lamb, the perfect sacrifice for our eternal redemption! Lean on this Lamb and the snake becomes helpless.

Read Aloud in Public

A proper reading of God's Word as written leads to basic under-standing of reality as it should be understood by the Christian believer. This understanding comes in story form, the greatest story ever told. It inspires a willingness to view all truth claims in the clarifying light of biblical revelation. This reality vision is what underlies all attempts at Christian worship, doctrine, and mission. Being and acting like a Christian requires seeing this world as the Bible presupposes that it really is.

Our present world is filled with conflicting visions. They influence and too often distort a Christian's thinking unless that believer knows well the biblical vision. Therefore, reading the book of God is so important. We are to read carefully and come to believe deeply.

Important as Bible reading is, so many Christians today are doing very little of it beyond short "devotions" that address life direction from a select Bible verse. While helpful, this isn't the comprehensive Bible reading and understanding that's needed by itself.

Much biblical material was originally for *public reading* to God's people who often were illiterate and had no direct access to the sacred text. Note Paul's instruction in Colossians 4:16 and the many other examples when key portions of the biblical text were read aloud. Most Christians are now literate and have access to the written Word. Even so, they rarely take adequate advantage of this privilege.

There is great need today for hearing the Word of God read aloud in the worship gatherings of God's people. We who believe in Jesus as Lord come together in worship to hear, learn, process as a body, and be inspired to obey. Much of the Bible's material was framed originally for such public and vocal conveyance. God's people need to hear and process the sacred text together. To be commended are the Christian congregations that regularly feature the reading of the Bible as a central feature of every worship service.

Use of a lectionary aids greatly in choosing selections of the biblical text appropriate for each Sunday, guiding a congregation through the entire Bible in a three-year cycle, with each set of readings fitting a season of the Christian Year (see the graphic above). Two extensive volumes guide in doing this, always quoting the thinking of Jesus to orient every engagement with any portion of God's written Word.[101]

Nevertheless!

A significant exposure to the Bible, whether by sight or ear and when interpreted according to its prime purposes, will lead to this critical question. Am I now prepared to receive and share what has been seen or heard? Coming to know biblical truth is intended to lead to personal transformation and then public proclamation and life expression.

The same people who were stunned mourners at the cross of Jesus soon were fearless witnesses across the land. Martin Luther and John Calvin in the sixteenth century are credited with sparking the Protestant Reformation. If here now, they likely would insist on having that put another way. Here's what really happened.

Luther began studying the written Word of God for himself and it began exploding inside him. Once exploding, he turned it loose on Germany. It was the same with Calvin in Switzerland, and later John Wesley in England. They agreed that there is enough undiscovered and unexperienced truth in the Bible to produce a spiritual awakening and church reformation in every generation. If only we will expose ourselves to the truth, the explosions will come.

All truth is God's truth from whatever source. Any supposed truth is to be judged as true only if it's in accord with the vision of truth biblically revealed. Will you make it yours and then turn it loose?

A great Scottish preacher read well the Bible's powerful message. He then announced this from his pulpit in Edinburgh, Scotland, as World War II raged in his nation. "The facts of life have a disconcerting way of confounding our careful theories, throwing out our calculations, contradicting our generalizations, embarrassing our precisions, and dynamiting our dogmatisms. *Nevertheless!*" (Heb 12:11; 2 Cor 7:5-6).[102]

When the Bible's end is reached, a "nevertheless!" is shaking the skies. The light of a new day is straining to shine for us. There is biblical talk of God making all things new. One contemporary Irish believer says this. "If you don't believe that the light is there, you always will experience the darkness. But if you believe and allow the light to come to you as it wishes, it will never fail you. I think that the heart of the Christian mystery, the resurrection of Jesus, means that at the heart of the darkness there isn't darkness but the *eternal candle*."[103]

The Bible ends with this. The Bright Morning Star says, "I'm on my way! I'll be there soon!" The faithful Bible reader should respond. "Yes! Come, Master Jesus!" (Rev 22:20). Meanwhile, as the Bible is read and the faith journey of believers proceeds with the Spirit's guidance, this should be the constant prayer:

> Flame within the fire, Breath within the breeze,
> Dove of highest heaven, come and dwell in me.
> Fill me with your perfect wisdom, calm my restless mind,
> Be my strength and consolation, Comforter divine.[104]

ENDNOTES

FOREWORDS AND PREFACE

1   Richard Rohr, *What Do We Do with the Bible?* 2021.

2   Richard Rohr, *Yes and . . . Daily Meditations,* 2019.

1:   AVOIDING THE TOXIC MIX

3   Consult works like Gordon D. Fee, *New Testament Exegesis,* 2002, and Joel B. Green, *Seized by Truth,* 2007.

4   Clark H. Pinnock and Barry L. Callen, *The Scripture Principle,* 2009.

5   Gilbert W. Stafford, *Theology for Disciples,* 2012.

6   See all this recounted and explained Barry L. Callen, *Bible Stories for Strong Stomachs,* 2017.

7   Good sources for the thinking of Roger Olson are *The Essentials of Christian Thought,* 2017, and *Against Liberal Theology,* 2022.

2:   BECOMING CAPTIVE

8   Joel B. Green, *Seized by Truth,* 2007.

9   David F. Watson, *Scripture and the Life of God,* 2017.

10   I prepared these volumes with the assistance of Steve Hoskins and Jonathan Powers.

11   Stanley J. Grenz, *Renewing the Center,* 2000.

12   George Kufeldt, in Barry Callen, ed., *Listening to the Word of God,* 1990.

13   E. R. Richards and B. J. O'Brien, *Misreading Scripture with Western Eyes,* 2013.

3: ONE RARE ISLAND

14 The amazing story of this isolated island and its few inhabitants is told by Adam Goodheart in *The Last Island,* 2023.

15 J. B. Phillips, *Your God Is Too Small,* 1952.

16 Robert Webber, *Ancient-Future Faith: Rethinking Evangelicalism for a Postmodern Generation,* 1999.

17 Cheryl Bridges Johns, *Re-enchanting the Text,* 2023.

18 Consult M. Robert Mulholland, *Shaped by the Word,* 2001.

19 Stanley J. Grenz, *Theology for the Community of God,* 1995.

20 Joel B. Green, *Seized by Truth,* 2007.

21 Cheryl Bridges Johns, *Re-enchanting the Text: Discovering the Bible as Sacred, Dangerous, and Mysterious,* 2023.

4: A SHIFTING EMPHASIS

22 Max Weber, *The Sociology of Religion,* 1922, 270.

23 See Walter Brueggemann, *The Word that Redescribes the World,* 2006, 6.

24 Richard Rohr, *What Do We Do with the Bible?,* 2021.

25 See Miroslav Volf, *Captive to the Word of God,* 2010.

26 Cheryl Bridges Johns, *Re-enchanting the Text,* 2023.

27 See this elaborated in Barry L. Callen, *Time to Think Again!* 2024.

28 Frederick Buechner, *Beyond Words,* 2004.

29 Eugene Peterson, *Eat This Book: A Conversation in the Art of Spiritual Reading,* 2006.

30 Cheryl Bridges Johns, *Re-enchanting the Text,* 2023.

31 James D. Smart, *The Strange Silence of the Bible in the Church,* 1970.

32 Cheryl Bridges Johns, *Re-enchanting the Text,* 2023.

33 Barry L. Callen, *Christian Holiness,* 2023.

34 Eugene H. Peterson, *Eat This Book,* 2006.

35 Alister McGrath, *A Passion for Truth,* 1996.

36 William J. Abraham, *Canon and Criterion in Christian Theology,* 1998.

37 Stanley J. Grenz, *Revisioning Evangelical Theology,* 1993.

38 This major shift of emphasis to God's intention was experienced by Clark Pinnock and is detailed in his biography by Barry L. Callen, *Journey Toward Renewal,* 2000.

39 Hymn title, "Break Thou the Bread of Life."

40 Cheryl Bridges Johns, *Re-enchanting the Text,* 2023. See the Aldersgate Press publication of Don Thorsen's book on God, *I Am Who I Am,* 2025.

41 Joel B. Green, in Richard Thompson and Barry Callen, eds., *Reading the Bible in Wesleyan Ways,* 133-134.

42 The writings of Marvin R. Wilson and Dwight A. Pryor have been most helpful to me in this regard.

43 See Barry L. Callen, *Caught Between Truths,* 2007.

44 See Robert E. Webber, *Ancient-Future Worship,* 2008, 130.

45 From "Come, Holy Ghost, our Hearts Inspire," in *The Book of Praise,* Presbyterian Church of Canada, 1972.

5: THE JOURNEY BEYOND WORDS

46 Joel B. Green, *Seized by the Truth,* 2007, chap. 1.

47 Marvin R. Wilson, *Our Father Abraham,* 1989.

48 Donald Bloesch, *The Holy Spirit: Works and Gifts,* 2000.

49 Joel B. Green, *Seized by Truth,* 2007.

50 Kallistos Ware, *The Orthodox Way,* 1995.

51 Eugene Peterson, Eat This Book, 2006.

52 *Lectio divina* is "divine reading," praying with the Scriptures while reading and meditating, contemplating, and finally praying. Common in monastic settings, something like it would be useful for many Protestant seekers after the fuller biblical truth.

53 Winn Collier, *A Burning in My Bones,* 2021.

54 Dallas Willard, *The Divine Conspiracy,* 1998.

55 See David R. Bauer and Robert A. Traina, *Inductive Bible Study,* 2014.

56 This summarization of *Lectio Divina* is by Don Marmion, O.S.B.

6:   THE ORIENTING THEMES

57   In his A Place to Stand, David Elton Trueblood identifies God in Christ as this solid center point of all truth.

58   Barry L. Callen, *God As Loving Grace,* 1996, 2018.

59   For a further elaboration of these four truth streams of the Bible, see Ronald Allen and John Holbert, *Holy Root, Holy Branches,* 1995, and Barry L. Callen, *Beneath the Surface,* 2012.

60   For a recent presentation of the various biblical dimensions of Christian holiness, see Barry L. Callen, Christian Holiness, 2023.

61   Christopher J. H. Wright, *The Old Testament in Seven Sentences,* 2021.

62   Thomas Merton, *Opening the Bible.* See Jeremiah 23:23-40.

7: THE WONDER OF IT ALL

63   Rufus M. Jones, *Studies in Mystical Religion,* 1909.

64   Barry L. Callen, *Authentic Spirituality,* 2006.

65   The author is Oswald Chambers.

66   T. Crichton Mitchell, *Charles Wesley: Man with the Dancing Heart,* 1994.

67   Barbara Brown Taylor, "A Great Cloud of Witnesses," in *Weavings* (Sept./Oct., 1988).

68   Barry L. Callen, *Authentic Spirituality,* 2006.

69   Words from the hymn "Grace Greater than Our Sin" by Julia Johnston.

70   Annie Johnson Flint, "He Giveth More Grace."

71   Barry L. Callen, *Authentic Spirituality,* 2006.

72   Lyrics by Albert W. T. Orsborn.

8:   A SURPLUS OF MEANING

73   Barry L. Callen, in Richard Thompson and Barry Callen, eds., *Reading the Bible in Wesleyan Ways,* 2004

74   See a helpful discussion of the thought of Clark H. Pinnock by Andrew Ray Williams, *Boundless Love,* 2021.

75   Sharon Clark Pearson, "Women as Bible Readers and Church Leaders," in *Reading the Bible in Wesleyan Ways,* eds. Barry Callen and Richard Thompson, 2004.

76   See, for example, Barry L. Callen, *She Came Preaching,* 1992.

77   Joel B. Green, *Seized by Truth,* 2007.

78   Clark H. Pinnock and Barry L. Callen, *The Scripture Principle,* 258.

79   Barry L. Callen, *Beneath the Surface,* 2012.

80   Clark H. Pinnock and Barry L. Callen, *The Scripture Principle,* 222.

81   Donald G. Bloesch, *Holy Scripture,* 1994.

82   Clark H. Pinnock, in *Reading the Bible in Wesleyan Ways,* eds. Barry Callen and Richard Thompson.

9:   GUIDELINES OF INTERPRETATION

83   Nadine Pence Frantz, doctoral dissertation, University of Chicago, 1992.

84   John A. Sanders, *Canon and Community,* 1984.

85   David F. Watson, *Scripture and the Life of God,* 2017.

86   See M. Robert Mulholland, Jr., *Shaped by the Word,* 1985, and his *Invitation to a Journey,* 1993.

87   N. T. Wright, *On Earth as in Heaven,* 2022.

88   Barry L. Callen, *The Prayer of Holiness-Hungry People,* 2011.

89   Charles Wesley's hymn titled "And Can It Be that I Should Gain?"

10:   STANDING ON THREE LEGS

90   See especially Don Thorsen, *The Wesleyan Quadrilateral,* 2018.

91   Thomas C. Oden, *Classic Christianity,* 2009, his systematic theology.

92   Barry L. Callen, *Guide of Soul and Mind,* 1992.

93   William J. Abraham, in *Conversion in the Wesleyan Tradition,* Kenneth Collins and John Tyson, eds., 2001. See also Abraham's *Canon and Criterion in Christian Theology,* 2002.

94   John B. Cobb in Barry L. Callen, *Heart of the Matter,* 2016.

95   Thomas C. Oden, *In Search of Solitude,* 2010.

96   Roger E. Olson, *Reformed and Always Reforming,* 2007.

97   Malcolm Muggeridge, *Conversion,* 1988.

98   See chapters 11-13 of Barry L. Callen, *Approaching Theology,* 2015.

99   David Elton Trueblood, as in Barry L. Callen, *Heart of the Matter,* 2016.

11: SEEING WHAT IS THERE

100 Found in the Foreword to Muggeridge's *Jesus Rediscovered,* 1969.

101 Barry L. Callen, et al, *A Year with Rabbi Jesus,* vols. 1 and 2, 2021, 2022, and Callen, *All of God's Word for All of My Needs,* 2023.

102 James S. Stewart, *The Strong Name,* 1941.

103 John O'Donohue, *Walking in Wonder,* 2018.

104 Words of the hymn "A Prayer for Pentecost," lyrics by Pamela Stewart.

www.ingramcontent.com/pod-product-compliance
Lightning Source LLC
Chambersburg PA
CBHW071805090426
42737CB00012B/1961